The Good Crewman

By the same author

South Biscay Pilot (Adlard Coles Ltd)
Pilot Cards (Imrays)

In preparation

South France Pilot (Imrays)

Robin Brandon

The Good Crewman

Drawings by Tim Reeve

Adlard Coles Limited

Granada Publishing Limited
First published in Great Britain 1972 by Adlard Coles Limited
3 Upper James Street London W1R 4BP

Copyright © 1972 Robin Brandon
Second impression 1974

ISBN 0 229 11502 0

Printed in Great Britain by
Fletcher & Son Ltd
Norwich

This book is dedicated to Jan, my Wife and Mate

Acknowledgements

The author is very conscious of the large number of people who have helped directly and indirectly in the production of this book, from those who taught him to sail a number of years ago to those who have contributed to his knowledge, and to those who had a direct hand in the writing and publication.

In particular he would like to thank Jim Cooper, Ian Black, Judy Russell, Johnnie Dacre, Phoebe Mason and Robert Brandon for reading the manuscript and offering their valuable comments and corrections. My thanks also to Mrs Hillhouse who typed the manuscript and to Tim Reeve who did the drawings.

Contents

Acknowledgements   vi

Foreword   xi

Preface   xii

Introduction   xiii

1 **Preparation**   1
knowledge skills physical clothing equipment getting to
know about the yacht joining ship

2 **Getting Under Way**   8
weighing anchor slipping a mooring leaving a berth
slipping from a pile or another yacht stowing deck gear

3 **Making Sail**   17
preparation hoisting

4 **Under Way**   28
watches helmsmanship using the compass streaming
and handing the log heaving or casting the lead
assisting the navigator sailing at night seasickness

5 **Sail Trimming and Changing**   45
mainsail headsails heaving-to spinnaker

6 **Emergencies**   63
gales sinking at sea going aground man overboard

7 **Arrival in Harbour**   76
preparation furling sails anchoring berthing mooring
to a buoy mooring to piles warping ship

8 **Harbour Work**   100
harbour stow flags dinghy work yacht engines going
ashore

9 **Domestic** 112
    cooking   bunking   heads   washing and shaving
    housework deck work

10 **Behaviour** 118
    consideration for others personal cleanliness sleeping,
    eating and drinking habits dirty work obstruction
    skippers' bêtes noirs psychology women crew

11 **Other Rigs** 124
    gaff rig topsail bowsprit topmasts cutter rig yawls
    ketches schooners

12 **Leaving Ship** 131
    Customs leaving ship

Appendices
A Glossary of Nautical Terms 133
B Parts of a Yacht 163
C Knots 170
D Further Reading 174
E Clothing and Personal Equipment 175
F Watch Systems 180
G Sounding with Lead and Line 182
H Rules of the Road at Sea 185

Illustrations

1	Personal gear	3
2	Joining ship	5
3	Slipping a mooring	10
4	Leaving a dinghy on a mooring	11
5	Securing alongside	13
6	Coiling large lines	14
7	Coiling lines in the hand	15
8	Putting on headsails	19
9	Hoisting the mainsail	20
10	Swigging down halyards	22
11	Cleating lines	23
12	Coiling rope on a cleat	24
13	Making fast wire halyards	26
14	Collision courses	32
15	Taking bearings to avoid collision	33
16	Steering at night	37
17	Mesmerisation by the compass	37
18	Tacking orders	47
19	Gybing orders	47
20	Heaving-to	53
21	Spinnaker stowage	56
22	Spinnaker sheeting arrangements	56
23	Hoisting the spinnaker	57
24	Spinnaker gybe—dipping boom method	58
25	Spinnaker gybe—double ended boom	58
26	Spinnaker gybe—two booms	58
27	Lowering a spinnaker	60
28	Spinnaker in stops	61
29	Emergency hull repairs	67
30	Fothering a sail over a hole in the hull	67
31	Heeling a yacht to reduce her draft	70
32	Drying out when heeled	70
33	Anchors laid out to assist righting	70
34	Manoeuvring to pick up a man overboard	73
35	Anchor ready to drop	77
36	Lowering sails incorrectly	81

37	Braking anchor chain	82
38	Anchor fouled by its chain	82
39	Making chain fast on samson post	82
40	Checking anchor drag	84
41	Bow fender	84
42	Anchor tripping line	85
43	Lying to two anchors	85
44	Anchor cable weight	88
45	Anchor light and shape	89
46	Stern lines prepared to pass ashore	90
47	Putting lines on bollards	91
48	Drying out alongside	92
49	Berthing stern-to	94
50	Approaching a mooring	95
51	Heaving on lines	98
52	Dinghy handling	103
53	The devil in the bilge	108
54	Effect of propeller handing	109
55	Turning under power	109
56	Going ashore	111
57	The companionway pest	121
58	Stowage of personal gear	122
59	Hoisting a gaff mainsail	125
60	Lowering a gaff mainsail	127
61	Gaff cutter	129
62	Gaff yawl	129
63	Gaff ketch	129
64	Gaff schooner	129
65	The parts of a yacht	164–65
66	Boom	166
67	Bowsprit	167
68	Trysail	168
69	Spinnaker	169
70	Reef knot	172
71	Bowline	172
72	Figure of eight knot	172–73
73	Sounding with lead and line	173

Foreword

No one has really tried to define the Good Crewman, mainly because skippers are such individualists that they would never agree on the ideal qualities required by their crew. 'Common sense', 'patience', 'instant obedience', 'never seasick', 'sense of humour', 'good bar companion', would be some of the comments, but none really help the newcomer to yachting whose major worry is adapting himself to an environment that has no parallel with ordinary life, and is further confused by having a mystifying language of terms that make medicine seem simple.

A comprehensive guide for the newcomer to sailing has long been needed, not only for the novice, but also for the crusty old salt who now, at last, has an easy to read explanation of those vital, easily forgotten, everyday points upon which his crew will look to him for guidance and encouragement.

Robin Knox-Johnston

Preface

One evening last summer while walking with my wife along the quays at Dartmouth, looking at the various craft moored alongside, we remarked on the tremendous variation between one yacht and another in the way that their gear was stowed. This started a conversation which was later carried on over dinner in a nearby restaurant. Examples were remembered of other yachts seen in an unseamanlike condition, of crews and even skippers behaving in a dangerous and foolish way, of the damage, injury and sometimes loss of life caused by such behaviour. We came to the conclusion that much of this poor standard of seamanship was of recent origin and could be to a great extent attributed to the vast increase in the number of yachts during the last decade manned by skippers and crews who are inexperienced and lack seamanlike knowledge. It is not unknown for a skipper to purchase his dream boat, acquire anyone as crew and set off, it might be said to learn the hard way, but in fact to learn the dangerous way.

This conversation developed into a discussion as to what could be done to improve this standard without the introduction of legislation, tests and licences, which are an anathema to yachtsmen. It was agreed that there are a number of training establishments doing a fine job in spreading knowledge, that there are a considerable number of books covering navigation and allied subjects and a certain number of books covering in outline the whole subject of yachting. What appeared to be lacking was any book that dealt with the job of crewing in detail for a crew member to read before his first voyage, which would contain enough basic information to enable him to become, with practice, what is any skipper's ideal—a 'good crewman'.

Robin Brandon
Salcombe

Introduction

This book is written for the reader who has had little or no experience of crewing in a cruising yacht. Perhaps the experienced crew also will find something that he or she had not thought of before, or learn some different way of doing a routine job. It is a time honoured principle that a skipper should be able to do all he asks his crew to do, and preferably better if he is to exercise effective command. Much that follows is common knowledge to the really experienced skipper, but there are others who by virtue of their own lack of training may find it of value.

There are many different ways of doing the same task on a yacht and the choice lies with the skipper. If every possible way of doing every job was included in a book such as this it would end up being very large and expensive. The author has in each case detailed what he considers to be the best methods based on a number of years of experience. The reader may find that his skipper prefers a different method, in which case he will have to receive instructions from him.

The good crewman has a personality that enables him or her to live and work under strange conditions, often uncomfortable, without clashing with the skipper or other members of the crew. He must have the knowledge to do his job efficiently; he must be fit and strong enough to carry on over a period of time; he must have the experience to back up his skipper in an emergency and to relieve him at other times. Of course other factors come into the picture. An offbeat crew member who is acceptable on a weekend cruise might cause a mutiny in a transatlantic passage, or a tough and tactless foredeck hand accustomed to a crack ocean racer might be an uncomfortable companion in a small weekend cruiser.

Of these four basic requirements the personality factor is perhaps the most important in cruising for pleasure. Few skippers will put up with failure in this direction, but any good skipper will do his best to remedy a lack of the other virtues. There are some skippers of the hearty, seadog type who learned their lessons in their youth with the help of a loud-mouthed mate and adjectival expletives, and see no problem that cannot be solved in the same fashion. At the other end of the scale there are those inexperienced in the ways of the sea who cannot accept that a powerful motor yacht is any different from an expensive motor car. There are some sadder and wiser yachtsmen alive today who would refute both of these theories.

The strange, restrictive, moving environment of a yacht at sea accompanied by unaccustomed powerful forces and strange noises tends to upset even those who have met it before. It is all part of acquiring what is called 'sea legs', which in its broadest sense is more than being able to balance the body with the movement of the ship. It also includes balancing the mind to the new environment. It can be a shattering experience to the unprepared crew member on his or her first voyage, and it is better to be prepared in advance.

The reader may get the impression that life on a small yacht is full of problems and hardships. This is not so as there will be many hours of pleasant and uneventful sailing very occasionally spiced with moments of excitement.

1 Preparation

Preparation carries its own reward. A crew member who has done all that he can to prepare himself will be certain to enjoy the voyage very much more, and at the same time stands a much better chance of being invited to crew again.

Preparation for a first voyage falls into the following divisions: *knowledge, skill, physical, equipment* and, not to be forgotten, *psychological.* Obviously no skipper will expect too much from a crew member on his first trip, but if he can join with some knowledge plus basic equipment, normal fitness, a determination to be as pleasant as possible and a desire to learn the ways of the owner and his yacht with eyes and ears open and a quiet tongue, the first important steps will have been taken.

Knowledge

This book has been written in the form of a narrative of a cruise to a foreign port and home again. The study of this book is all that is required of a novice before his first trip, but if time permits the attendance at lectures covering basic navigation and seamanship, the reading of any books devoted to similar subjects, and the perusal of any or all of the many magazines on yachting will all tend to impart background information so essential for the full enjoyment of the sport (see Appendix D for a bibliography).

On the subject of knowledge do not forget that you may have some knowledge that will be invaluable to your skipper, so if you are an expert on engines, radio, electrical apparatus, or you possess special skills such as carpentry, always let him know.

Skills

Prior to your first trip it is obvious that you are not going to be able to practice many skills as most of these are only acquired afloat. There are, however, two knots, the reef knot and bowline, that you should practice until you are perfect, and this means able to tie them in the dark at a moment's notice. The only way to do this is to tie them over and over again in all possible positions until you can be certain of always making them correctly (see Appendix C).

Physical

All that can be advised is to make every effort to get as fit as you can. It is certain that the voyage will be very much more pleasant if you are fit and able to do your fair share of the work. Any exercise that will increase the bending, lifting and pulling muscles and harden the hands will be of great value. However, it is not necessary to become a he-man (or woman) in order to become a good crewman.

Clothing

There is a list in Appendix E of personal clothing that a crewman should take aboard. The list also includes the special items required by men and women. Clothing is naturally very much a matter of personal taste, but a novice would be ill advised not to have any of the items listed in the 'must' section. Some of the items in this section, particularly oilskins, are expensive to buy and for a first voyage efforts could be made to borrow from a friend, or it may be worth while to check with your skipper to see if he has a spare set aboard that you could use. Obviously these lists would have to be modified if the voyage were to be a long one, or to a region where the climate was different. Another factor to consider is the standard of dress demanded by the skipper.

1 *Never bring your gear on board in large suitcases. Irate skippers have been known to throw them overboard. There is no place to stow them on a normal yacht*

Most crew on their first trip are amazed by the restricted stowage space on a normal yacht. They must therefore make every effort to reduce the amount of gear that they take aboard to an absolute minimum. Experience shows us that in almost every case people will always bring much more on board than they really require (58).

One of the greatest crimes is to arrive with a hard suitcase of large size. Irate skippers have been known to throw them over the

B

side. Never pack your gear in suitcases no matter how small, but always use a soft kit bag or grip that can be bundled up and stuffed away in the back of a small locker (1, 58).

A great boon to small-boat sailors in recent years is the plastic bag. A good supply of these should be taken and all clothing kept in them, but do not throw them overboard where they clog up engine inlets, foul propellers and litter beaches.

Another problem is the limited amount of water available and the very restricted washing facilities. It may not be possible to do any laundry work, therefore adequate supplies of underclothes, etc. should be taken.

Clothing is liable to be damaged or get wet with salt water, so do not take anything that you particularly value which would be ruined in this way.

Equipment

The amount of equipment that a crew member requires is small and a list of items is to be found in Appendix E. Cameras are very susceptible to damage both from salt water and by mischance. Valuable items should always be kept stowed in plastic bags in a secure place and replaced there immediately after use.

It is advisable to check with the skipper whether he wants you to bring a radio. Most yachts are equipped with a special receiver and also a normal broadcast set. A third radio is rather overdoing things on a small yacht!

Getting to know about the yacht

It is a great advantage to find out the likes and dislikes of your skipper and crew *before* you join the yacht. It may be that you already know them well. In this case much of what is written below is of no consequence to you. However, an hour or so discussing the forthcoming trip with him will be worth several days at sea and you will have a head start. If you do not know the skipper and crew find out what their attitude is to cleanliness, tidiness, drinking, behaviour ashore and afloat. Find out if you are required to contribute money to a 'kitty'; if you should bring food, drink or some gift; if it is usual to dine the skipper out for a meal, or any other similar arrangements. Each ship and skipper will have their own arrangements and it is up to the crew to find out what they are because most skippers are notoriously bad at disseminating this type of information. A few direct questions over the phone, or in a letter to the skipper, should enable you to form some ideas as to what is required.

2   *If you are joining the yacht by car let the skipper know. You may be able to help by bringing down other crew members or gear*

It is vital that you must find out, with no possibility of error, exactly where and when you are required to join the ship and to allow yourself extra time to cater for any eventualities. A new crew member arriving late and causing his skipper to miss a tide will never be forgiven. If you are driving to join the yacht you may be able to give a lift to another crew member, which is a good opportunity to find out the form. You may be able to take some gear down with you so let your skipper know how you plan to travel (2).

Your skipper should also be asked if there is any special personal gear and equipment he would like you to bring along. Normally the lists in Appendix E should suffice, but he may have some plan or invitation that necessitates some special form of dress. It is fairly common practice for a skipper to have a duplicate letter sent to each crew member a few days before joining, giving full details of the proposed cruise and what will be required.

Joining ship

The great moment is on hand. You have travelled down to the prearranged rendezvous and have arrived with time to spare. Have a good look round and if any yachtsmen or fishermen are to be seen ask them to point out your skipper's yacht. Perhaps the harbour master or some other knowledgeable person may be near by to ask about the yacht. If they are not too busy you may get some valuable information.

If you are joining ship in a large commercial port allow even more time as it may be difficult to track down the exact basin where the yacht is lying. If she is lying in an estuary it may be a long distance from where you have to leave your car and you may have to organise some means of getting out to her. Never be afraid to ask questions of anyone remotely connected with yachting and the sea. You will be very pleasantly surprised at the friendly help you will always receive.

You will at last make contact with the yacht. If you are using a dinghy and have not been in one before, take care always to step into the middle and keep your weight as low as possible. If you step on the dinghy's gunwale (edge) it may capsize. Also watch out that you do not get your fingers pinched between the side of the dinghy and the quay or the yacht's hull. Never stand up in a dinghy or move about violently (52).

If by any chance you are wearing shoes with leather soles or studs remove them before going on board, and put on your deck shoes or remain in bare feet. Hard shoes can easily damage the wood and varnish work.

Once on board and having met your skipper and the other crew members your first task will be stow your gear and to organise your bedding. Personal clothing should be stowed carefully so that various items can be found with the minimum effort and delay, an important point when you are feeling seasick! Perhaps your skipper's intention is to get under way at once, in which case a quick change into sea-going gear is indicated before the open sea is reached. If, however, a more leisurely voyage is planned, your skipper may appoint an experienced crew member to show you over the yacht in detail (58). Now is the time when all those long hours of study will stand you in good stead, and when your guide starts to use technical terms you will have met them before. If, however, he uses a term with which you are not familiar never hesitate to ask for an explanation. As a good crewman you must know all the technical terms, and there are many which are used on board (Appendices A and B).

Perhaps a word of advice may be necessary to some at this stage: do not be too talkative; wait until you have been adopted as a crew member before giving rein to your prowess as wit and conversationalist.

2 Getting Under Way

Weighing anchor

At last the skipper has decided to get under way. A good skipper
will tell the crew in advance what his plan is for getting under way,
but this does not mean that he will always follow a plan without
variation if the situation changes. His novice crew is best employed
keeping his eyes open and his wits about him, learning what is done
and assisting where necessary, such as in helping to heave up the
anchor. When you have to use all your strength, such as on the
anchor cable, make sure that you are using it to full advantage and
are pulling with a straight back and nearly straight legs, also that
you are not pulling against another crew member (51).

When all the slack anchor chain has been pulled in the anchor
will be directly under the bows and whoever is in charge of the
foredeck will call out to the skipper 'Up and down', or make some
prearranged sign. When the anchor comes clear of the bottom,
which usually requires an extra hard pull, a cry of 'Anchor's
aweigh' or another signal is given. Care is now necessary in pulling
in the remainder of the cable as the anchor can damage the hull or
rail of the yacht as it comes aboard. Inexperienced hands have been
known to go on heaving on the chain with the flukes (points) of the
anchor firmly embedded in the hull! When the anchor is out of the
water a cry of 'Clear' is made or the appropriate sign used. Now
starts what is probably the most difficult task in anchor work,
which is getting the heavy awkwardly shaped anchor on deck
without damaging either the yacht or the crew. If the anchor is
dropped on deck by mistake it can do a fearful amount of damage

so take care. In some anchorages the anchor will come up covered in mud and it will be necessary either to scrub it clean with a deck broom as it clears the water, or where this is not possible, on deck. This mud is usually of a foul sticky nature and will cling to everything. Make sure that you, your hands, and the yacht are all quite clean before leaving the foredeck.

In most yachts the anchor stows in chocks on deck and usually is lashed in place. The reef knot will do here. The navel pipe where the chain passes through the deck may have a canvas cover to prevent water getting below. This must be put in place and securely tied. Some yachts have chain lockers in difficult places and the chain will not stow itself as it falls down the navel pipe. In this case one of the crew is detailed to go below to stow it as it comes aboard by flaking it from side to side in loose coils in its locker so it doesn't pile up.

While dealing with the chain the novice may notice that it is marked at intervals with paint or by some other method. When all is peace and quiet find out what these marks signify, because there is no accepted code for marking lengths on chain. Each yacht has its own system.

When there is a sea running, especially when handling heavy gear, watch your balance. If you can sit down to work, or wind your leg or arm around some support such as the mast, you are much more secure. It is ridiculously easy to fall overboard, and most yacht rails are at knee height, which is just right to catch you behind the legs and tip you over the side should you stumble. The age-old cry of 'one hand for the ship and one for yourself' still applies today.

From this first exercise in seamanship the new crew will observe that there are several basic principles. These are *efficiency, organisation, teamwork, safety of yacht and crew, prevention of damage, correct drill* and *cleanliness,* all of which are common to every activity carried out aboard.

Slipping a mooring

If the yacht is lying to a mooring buoy you will find slipping a mooring much more simple than anchor work. On a small yacht all that is necessary is to untie *one* end of the mooring line, hold it in your hand or with half a turn round a cleat, make sure that it will run free, and indicate to the skipper that all is ready to slip (3). When ordered to slip, let go smartly and, most important, get the line aboard quickly before it drags under the boat. It is very easy for ropes which have been allowed to hang over the side of a yacht to be caught by the propeller, which will wind them round and round into a terrible tangle and more often stop the ship at the most

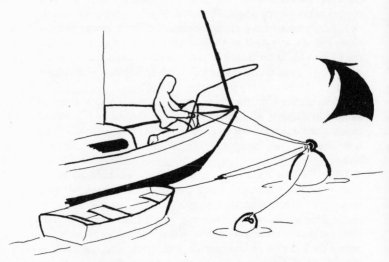

3 *A yacht may be secured to a mooring with a short length of chain which is connected to the rising chain from the mooring. There may be a pick-up buoy on a short length of line on the other end. This buoy is normally lashed to the forestay and must be put over the side before the mooring is slipped.*

awkward moment. The only way to clear this snarl-up is for someone to go over the side and cut it free under water, which is not a pleasant or popular pastime.

Larger yachts will be lying to a mooring with a chain which may or may not be a part of the yacht's gear. In both cases a short heavy line or mooring rope is passed through the mooring eye and both ends of this line secured on board. The chain is then unshackled and stowed or left on the mooring as required. The yacht is now riding to the line. When ready to slip, the procedure is as with the smaller yacht, explained above. Some buoys have smaller pick-up buoys attached to the large mooring buoy by a short length of rope. When on a mooring of this type the small buoy is lashed to the forestay and must obviously be put over the side before slipping. In all work dealing with chains and lines it is vital to make sure that they will run free and have not been lead the wrong side of stanchions, stays, rails, or any fixed point that might trap them as they are running out (35, 46).

4   *If the dinghy is tied to the mooring buoy on too short a scope (length of line) it may be difficult to bring the yacht up to the mooring without running over the dinghy*

The skipper may want to leave his tender (dinghy) on the mooring while the yacht is away, in which case its painter (bow rope) must be made fast to the mooring buoy. A bowline will do for this knot, though later you will learn several others that are better. Tie it in a big bight (loop) so that it can be untied from deck level, but do not tie it on too short a scope (length) as on his return the skipper may not be able to bring the bow of the yacht up to the mooring without running over the dinghy (4). Make sure that there are no trailing ropes to catch the propeller and that the oars are secure inside the dinghy so that they cannot fall out should a sea

11

get up during your absence. Once again the job is not finished until all the lines on deck are coiled down and all gear put away, leaving everything clean and tidy.

Many yachts today have inflatable dinghies, and these are usually taken on board. Sometimes they are deflated, folded and stowed in their bags below, at other times they are only half deflated, folded to reduce their bulk, and lashed on deck. They are simple to operate and safe to use, but when out of water they can catch the wind and blow over the side.

No mention has been made of the boat hook in the previous paragraphs in order to keep the drill as simple as possible. This piece of gear is most valuable and should always be unlashed and ready to hand when dealing with anchors and moorings. A boat hook requires practice to use efficiently, and care must be taken when using it not to cause damage if it has a sharp spike. Boat hooks have an annoying habit of slipping over the side. If this happens and it is entirely your fault do not forget to offer to buy another for your skipper. He will probably refuse the offer. Naturally you should also offer to replace any other items of the ship's gear that you personally lose or damage through carelessness.

Leaving a berth

You may find that the yacht is secured alongside a quay or jetty by lines, in which case the necessary drill is even more simple. The yacht will normally be secured with bow and stern lines, springs and breast lines, with fenders between the side of the yacht and the quay wall (5). The skipper will, depending on the strength and direction of the wind and tidal currents, order these various lines to be singled down (reduced) to the one or two that he wishes to be released last. These selected lines should first be doubled so that both ends are secured on board the yacht and they run free around a bollard or ring on the quay. When this has been done the remaining lines are slipped and brought on board, if possible without dragging them in the dirt or the water, and coiled away. Now make quite sure that those left are ready to slip and that they will catch on nothing as they run. On the command 'Slip' let go *one* end and haul in the other handsomely (carefully), getting the bitter end (far end) on board and clear of the propeller as soon as possible.

The skipper may ask you to fend off at this stage as the wind or current may be setting the yacht onto the wall. Push firmly and steadily against the wall and do not expect any immediate result. Yachts are heavy things and require considerable effort to move them, and once moving to stop them. The leg has powerful muscles and if used intelligently is better than arms, but take care not to get limbs trapped or overbalance and fall in the water. Keep your eyes and wits about you to see what your crew mates are doing and do not, as so often happens, work against them.

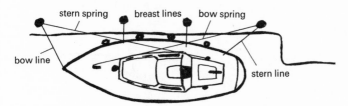

5   *The yacht will be secured alongside the quay with bow and stern lines, bow and stern springs and two breast lines. Fenders are hung over the side between the hull and the quay wall to protect the hull*

Once away from the wall get the fenders inboard smartly and stowed, making quite sure that nothing has been missed. A yacht leaving harbour with a line trailing or a fender over the side is the butt of jokes and comment from any seaman that sees it. The skipper will not be pleased to hear about it from his friends on his return to port.

Slipping from a pile or another yacht

If by chance your yacht is moored to a pair of piles (large posts) and is, as is often done, secured alongside another yacht, a similar procedure to that detailed in the section above is carried out. It is possible that a crew member may have to go to the piles in the dinghy to free or untie the bow and stern lines. These have a nasty habit of being under water when the skipper decides to leave, often with other yachts' badly tied lines on top to make the job more

13

difficult. Naturally more care has to be taken when slipping from the other yacht, and the boat hook, if used, must be placed where it can do no damage, especially if it has a sharp point. The butt end can be used in some circumstances if it can be placed where it will not slip under pressure.

Stowing deck gear

Lines and warps are difficult things to coil down unless you know the correct way to do it (6). First make sure that you have the line

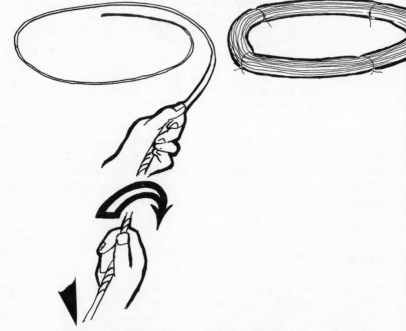

6 *As you coil a heavy line down on the deck give it a clockwise twist, which will cause it to lie flat without kinks. When a long, heavy line is fully coiled down pass at least four lashings of small stuff (light rope) around it to stop it uncoiling*

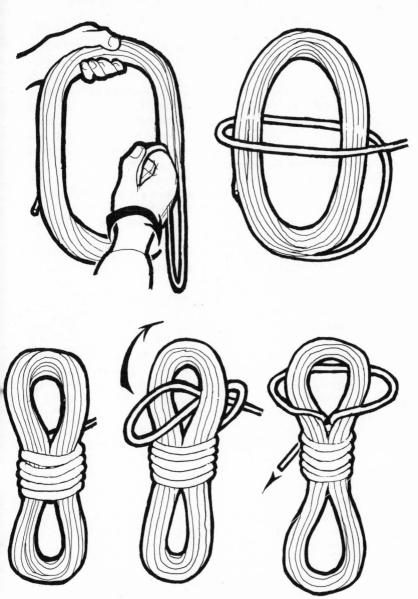

7 As you coil a line in your hand give each turn a clockwise
twist, to cause it to lie relaxed in its coil. When you reach the
end leave about a metre over, wind this two or three times
around the outside of the coil, make a bight (loop) with the
remainder, and pass it through the top of the coil and back
over the outside. Pull the end tight

free at each end and loosely flaked down (laid out) on the deck. Take the top free end and start to make a clockwise coil about one metre in diameter on deck clear of obstructions, continue coiling giving a clockwise twist to the rope with each turn on deck so that it lies relaxed in its coil. If a second crew member feeds the rope to you while twisting it clockwise at the same time, the job can be completed in half the time. When completely coiled pass at least four lashings of small stuff (short lengths of thin rope) spaced equally around the sides and tied with a reef knot.

Smaller and lighter lines can be coiled in the hand (7). In this case, if right handed, again coil clockwise with your right hand into your left, giving a clockwise twist to each turn. The size of the coil will be decided by the amount of rope that you gather for each turn with your right hand. When completed the coil can be lashed in the same manner as the larger coil, or the end of the line itself may be used for this purpose. In this case, when you have almost completed the coil allow yourself about one metre over, pass this around the whole coil several times, then form a loop in what remains and pass it through the top of the coil just under your left hand, pulling it back over the outside of the top of the coil. Lines and warps are usually stowed in the forepeak and may be on pegs specially labelled for the purpose. Fenders are normally stowed with the lines. Give these a quick look over before passing them below as they may have collected some oil from the harbour wall and this must first be removed.

A task which is often allocated to the junior crew member is preparing and hoisting the burgee. This flag is normally attached to a short staff and hoisted to the top of the mast by means of the burgee halyard. The staff is attached to its halyard by two clove hitches, one near the bottom of the staff and the other at the middle. When hoisting endeavour to stand downwind of the mast so it does not foul the rigging as it is hoisted. A small flip on the halyard when the flag is level with the top of the mast will usually take it clear of the standing rigging. When hoisted cleat and stow the falls.

3 Making Sail

Preparation

Somewhere on board will be stowed the headsails, usually in the forepeak and in sail bags. These bags should be marked with a code to show which sails they contain. The more normal codes are colours or numbers. A list of the sails and the relevant code is often stuck up near the sail bins. (The main is normally left on its boom with a cover over it.) If a sail has been properly stowed in its sail bag the tack will have been left on top and ready to be pulled out, as this is the first part of the sail that is required. The skipper will have chosen a suitable headsail and it must be got on deck together with the correct sheets, which are to be found nearby. On most yachts the sheets must be lead outside the rigging and rails, and then through the sheet block direct to the winch, with a thumb or figure eight knot tied in the end to prevent it slipping back through the block (Appendix C, 72). Check, as always, to see if they will run free and are rove (put through blocks) in the correct manner. It is very easy to lead them the wrong side of the rails or rigging.

Tie the sail bag to a guardrail near the bow so that it cannot blow away and pull the first part of the sail out, being careful that it does not take charge and blow over the side. Get hold of the tack (lower, forward corner) and shackle it to its correct point at the bow. Be sure that it is the right way up and that the edge which has the hanks is above the tack and in the bow. Hank the sail on starting at the bottom and working upwards, following the edge of the sail so as not to miss any and make sure that piston type hanks are closed.

The hanks must all be put on facing the same direction, otherwise the luff will be twisted when hoisted. It is easier to hank on headsails with one crewman passing the sail forward to another, who sits in the bow or pulpit facing aft. When the hoist (top) is reached, find the appropriate headsail halyard and its falls (its opposite end). Take it off its cleat and make sure not to let the falls go free. If they are allowed to slip they will run up the mast at the first opportunity and the only way to get them down is for someone, you for preference, to be hoisted to the top of the mast to recover them! Shackle the halyard to the head making certain that the halyard is not twisted around the forestay, and that it has a clear run direct to the halyard block at the top of the mast. A point to note when working with a shackle: always take great care not to drop it or its pin. If you do they will slide across the deck and overboard in a flash. The pin must be screwed home with a marlinspike or shackle key or it will unscrew, usually at the wrong moment. You may have to change sails in the dark and in strong winds, and from the foregoing it will be seen why it is important to stow headsails with the tacks uppermost.

The sheets must now be shackled on. Follow the foot of the sail from the tack at the bow to the clew to see that it is not twisted. Now check that the sheets have not become twisted and shackle them to the sail. All is now ready, so tell your skipper that the headsail (foresail or jib) is ready to hoist. If he does not want it right away he will want it lashed down so it will not be blown or washed over the side. Take a long sail tie (a length of webbing or rope), pass it through the three shackles at the three corners of the sail and pull them together; then use the rest of the tie to lash the belly of the sail into a small neat bundle on the pulpit or rail clear of the deck. A more attractive way is to have the clew as far aft as possible and lash the sail along the rail, making sure the head is tied down and the halyard kept taut and cleated.

Now for the mainsail. First the cover must be taken off. It is possible to roll the cover along the top of the sail, making a nice neat bundle for stowage. Some skippers leave the battens in the sail, others insist that they are removed when the sail is furled, in which case the sail will have to be unlashed and they must be put in their correct pockets, the battens and the sail pockets being numbered from top to bottom.

The halyard must be shackled securely to the hoist of the sail

8 *Be careful to shackle and hank on the headsail(s) the correct way up. The skipper will not be pleased if when he orders it to be hoisted it is found to be the wrong way up!*

after a check to see that it has a clear run to the halyard block and that the falls are also clear and secure. The main sheets are now freed and overhauled (pulled out through the blocks) so that when the sail is hoisted the boom is free to swing. Next the topping lift must be cast off its cleat and the boom topped up so that it is clear of its crutch or gallows and so that when the sail is hoisted the weight of the boom is taken on the topping lift and not on the sail itself. The boom crutch or gallows is now removed and stowed (9).

Again, if the skipper does not want to hoist the sail right away sail ties are passed around the sail and boom to keep it under control. Watch out for the boom swinging about if the sheets are left free. It is easy to be caught unawares and perhaps be knocked overboard or at least to receive a nasty bang.

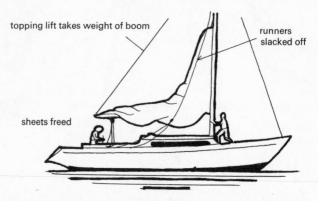

topping lift takes weight of boom

runners slacked off

sheets freed

9   *Before hoisting the mainsail, the leeward topping lift and running backstays, if fitted, must be slack. The mainsheet must be pulled out through its blocks so that the boom can swing out, and the sail ties cast off. While hoisting it helps if a crewman pulls the leech aft to guide it away from spreaders and any other obstruction*

All the tasks just described can be carried out by one crew member, but working as a team of two or three the job can be done much more efficiently. With the foresail, for example, one crew member sits in the pulpit facing aft, shackles the tack and hanks on the sail as it is handed to him section by section by a second member, and the third man reeves the sheets and attaches them to the clew. In this way the sail will be ready very quickly, but extra care is necessary when working as a team to see that the sail does not get twisted.

Some craft may have some special fittings or gear which will require attention. For example, there may be twin forestays in which case the hanks must be put on one stay only. If the sail is 'cross hanked' onto both stays it will jam. There may be twin topping lifts, in which case only the windward lift is topped up. The other is left slack so that it does not foul the mainsail when it is hoisted. Many yachts have running backstays and in this case the leeward one is released before hoisting the mainsail.

There are various types of halyard; the simplest, found on small craft, is a single length of rope or sometimes rope tailed to wire. This rope is made fast to a cleat on the mast. Others have small winches on the mast or on deck nearby which are used to set up the halyards really tight. Others again have a wire halyard the falls of which are wound up on a special winch. There are even more complicated methods such as the two-piece tackle where as a first stage a lanyard pulls a single block down to the deck where it is hooked in, hoisting the sail at the same time. The halyard proper is rove through this block to another block which is attached via a short wire strop to the hoist of the sail and this second stage is used to sweat up the sail. This gives extra power without recourse to halyard winches. There will be cleats specially intended for each halyard and it is important that each halyard should always be put down on to its correct place as it may have to be cast loose in a hurry in the darkness.

The best advice to the inexperienced crew is to have a very careful look at all of the running gear and make certain what it is used for and how it is used before leaving port. Try to memorise these details.

Hoisting

We now come to the drills for hoisting sails. The skipper will decide which sail he wants hoisted first and will let the crew know by the order 'Hoist main (headsail/foresail/jib)' or by a suitable sign. To divert for a moment, it is far better to have a series of agreed simple signs for communication between skipper and crew than to have people bawling out orders which may or may not be heard above the noise of the wind and waves, to say nothing of the noise of flapping sails. An efficient and experienced skipper will conduct all the various drills and manoeuvre a yacht in almost perfect silence. It is always easy to pick out the novice skippers and crews by the shouts and yells that accompany every activity.

Main

If possible the skipper will steer the yacht into the wind while the main is being hoisted. This makes the job very easy for the crew as it minimises the chance of the sail fouling any of the rigging. If, however, he cannot do this it is most important to see that the mainsheet is overhauled and freed so that the boom can swing out, and if the yacht is rigged with double topping lifts and/or running backstays, that those on the leeward side are as slack as possible (9). This entails a certain amount of preplanning on the part of the skipper, who should let the crew know which side will be to windward when he plans to have the sails hoisted. Now cast off the remaining sail ties and hoist away smartly. While doing this watch the sail to see if it catches on anything (9). It can easily foul the

10 *To take up the slack in a halyard fall, swig it down. Pass the fall under a cleat and while holding this fast pull the fall away from the mast, and then downwards while taking in the slack around the cleat with the other hand. Two crew working together can do this more efficiently*

topping lifts, backstays, shrouds and crosstrees (spreaders). When pulling on or paying out a rope never fail to watch what the other end is doing. The natural inclination is to watch your hands, and many sails have been torn by inexperienced crew failing in this respect (36). This is a most important rule.

If there are two of you hoisting the main, the second man should be pulling the leech aft and guiding it clear of any possible obstructions. An extra hand tailing on the halyard as it leaves the winch will speed hoisting. When the sail is up it will be necessary to get the luff tight. Without a winch this is best done by sweating up (also called swigging down) the halyards (10). Make a half turn around the cleat to jam the fall, then with the other hand pull the halyard away from the mast and then downwards, taking in any slack gained by pulling it around the cleat. Repeat the process several times until you can get no more slack. Cleat the halyard and make up the rest of the falls around the cleat. With two crew, one pulling and the other taking up the slack, a better result can be obtained. When fully sweated up report 'Main hoisted' or signal accordingly.

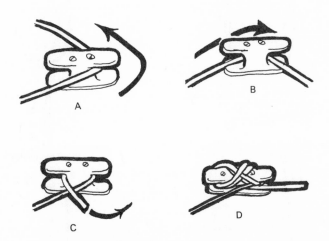

11 *A rope must lead clear to the* far *end of a cleat (A) and* not *to the nearer side (B) as it might jam. After one complete turn (C) the rope is made up in a figure eight pattern (D) and final half-hitch around the cleat if required*

There is only one correct way of making up on a cleat (11). Take the rope to the far end of the cleat clear of the cleat itself, pass it once round the whole cleat and then do several zig-zag crossing turns. With natural fibre rope never put a half round turn knot on top of this as it will jam when wet and you will not be able to lower the sails. Some skippers will, however, permit a half turn with ropes of a large size of man-made fibre. A better way is to take one more complete turn around the base of the cleat to jam the rope behind the zig-zag turns.

The best and neatest way to deal with the rope left over is to coil

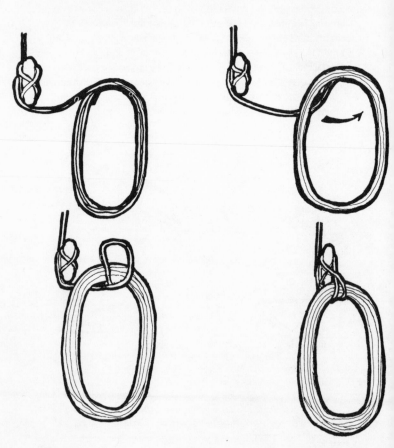

the balance into a smallish coil, hold it in your left hand, pass your right hand through this coil, grasp the rope just short of the cleat and pull a loop back through the coil, give it a half turn and place it over the top of the cleat (12). This sounds complicated but with a little practice it will be found very quick and easy to do. Some yachts have a permanent lashing with a wooden toggle and loop of rope fixed near the mast for the halyard falls, which is another neat and good method. Never adopt the unseamanlike, untidy practice of jamming the falls behind the halyard; they will be difficult to get out in a hurry and will tangle.

Your yacht may have a halyard winch. If it is of the open type a couple of turns round the barrel is all that is necessary at first, but when the full weight of the sail comes on the halyard and you want to get it up tight, about six turns will be necessary. Help from someone tailing or pulling steadily on the rope as it leaves the barrel of the winch will be of great assistance. When the mainsail is fully up, wind the rest of the wire falls around the winch barrel. Finally take the rope part of the falls and make them up round a cleat as before (13). It is most important that the wire or its splice should not be made up around a cleat in a sharp bend as it will damage the wire.

Halyard wire must never be kinked or bent sharply as this weakens it considerably. If the yacht has a halyard winch that winds up the falls it is only necessary to see that the turns go down smoothly side by side along the drum and that the brake is functioning correctly so that it can be released when the skipper wants the main lowered.

Some yachts will have a boom that can be varied in height. In this case when hoisting the main it helps if a second crew member lifts the boom from the mast end when the sail is almost fully up, thereby allowing the man on the halyard to winch the sail to the top of the mast. When the halyard is secured the boom is pulled down

12 *To make up the falls of a rope on a cleat make them into a neat coil, pass your hand through the centre of this coil and grasp the rope where it leads from the cleat to the coil, pull a bight (loop) back through the coil, give it a half twist and slip it over the top of the cleat. If the twisted bight is too short the rope will be too crowded to stay on the cleat; if it is too long the coil will be held only slackly, and come adrift*

by means of a small block and tackle under the boom at the mast end until the luff of the sail is taut. The next job is to slack away the topping lift so that the whole weight of the boom is on the sail, not forgetting to make up the falls. In modern yachts there may also be another tackle which runs from further aft under the boom to the foot of the mast and is called a kicking strop. This must also be pulled up tight and the best way to do this is for the mainsheet to be pulled in tight at the same time.

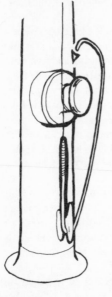

13   *When the sail has been fully winched up pass the remaining wire halyard falls around the barrel of the winch. If there is too much wire pass it under a cleat and back to the barrel. Make sure that the splice between the wire and the rope tail does not bend sharply around the winch barrel or cleat*

If there is a wind blowing when you hoist the sails for the first time do not be alarmed by the noise caused by the flogging sails; all is well and they will come to no harm.

Headsail

Hoisting the headsail is simple once you have mastered the main. The points to watch out for: make sure that the sail is not fouling anything as it is hoisted; keep clear of the clew as it flogs about, as a crack on the head from the sheet shackle can hurt; do not pull in the sheets and trim the sail until the halyard is up tight and secure, when a cry or sign can be made to the skipper that the headsail is hoisted. Unlike the main, the headsail can be hoisted with the wind in any direction, but if it is blowing from aft of the beam assistance from another crew member may be necessary to prevent it fouling the forestay as it is hoisted.

26

Finally carry out a careful check to see that all is correct and secure, that all running gear can be cast off without trouble and that all ropes are lead correctly.

Now that the sails are hoisted the skipper will order the sheets to be hauled in, and as the sails fill the flogging will cease and the yacht, feeling the wind, will heel over and start to move. There may be horrid sounds of things falling over down below because someone has forgotten to stow gear securely. Do not let it be your gear that was not stowed properly! Another thing often forgotten in the rush to get away is to shut and secure hatches, portholes and other openings, so the first seas that are shipped find their way below, usually over someone's bunk and clothing. While working on deck do your best to keep out of the skipper's line of sight. He will want a clear view forward to avoid obstructions and other craft.

4 Under Way

We are presuming, for the purpose of this book, that you are going to cross the Channel and visit a foreign port, so here we are under sail, the skipper having switched off the engine, leaving the shelter of the harbour. Naturally the first thing that will strike the novice is the movement and it will take him several days to become fully adjusted to this. At first he must move around slowly with care making sure that he has a least one hand on some secure place. At the same time he should not tense himself up unnecessarily. If you have to do some work outside the cockpit which requires you to use both hands it is best to sit down on the deck and wind your legs around some strong point.

Watches

The skipper if he is wise will put his watch system into use directly he leaves the coast, so do not be surprised if you are asked to go straight to your bunk. There are many and varied watch systems which can be used and some of these are listed in Appendix F. As sailing yachts are not fast, it will take some time to get across the Channel, so relax and have lots of patience. Never ask your skipper when he expects to arrive; he will not know as your speed is controlled by the strength and direction of the wind which he will not be able to forecast with any accuracy, but rest content that provided all goes well you will arrive in due course.

When you go to your bunk do not undress except for removing your oilskins if you are wearing them and your boots or shoes, as you may be required on deck in a hurry later. Sometimes, however, in good settled conditions and with a full crew your skipper may allow the crew to undress and bed down normally. The first thing that will strike you lying in your bunk below is the multitude of noises that the ship makes as she ploughs through the sea. There is the noise of the waves hitting the sides of the ship, the sound of trickling water as it runs off the deck, the sound of the hull itself, its creaks and groans. There are the sounds of loose gear, especially in the galley, sliding back and forth as the boat rolls. The sound of the wind in the rigging and a slack rope or block that bangs on the deck with every wave adds to the cacophony. Above all this there are the noises made by the watch on deck who will talk in loud voices to each other or move over the deck with heavy feet oblivious to the disturbance that they are causing below. Many of these noises can and should be prevented and others reduced, but the novice must realise that a yacht at sea is noisy below.

Half awake, you may hear a part of a remark made by someone on deck about the close approach of another ship or some other danger. Do not worry, as the skipper will call you on deck in good time if it is necessary. Relax and enjoy your rest.

When you are called to take your turn on deck watch get up at once, because the watch that you are relieving, who are probably cold and tired, will be justifiably annoyed if you are late. If you take longer than the average person to get up or will require more than one call tell the watch that is going to call you. Do not forget to leave your bunk and gear stowed before you go on deck. If gear is left lying around it will find its way onto the floor and will quickly get wet and dirty.

Sometimes the watch below may be divided in two, one half fully dressed on immediate call, the other half off duty and turned in. In this case, if short-handed on deck, a light rope tied around the shoulders of the fully dressed crew member can be led into the cockpit so that the helmsman can get help by pulling on the rope to waken this standby crew member and get him on deck when required.

Watch on deck

The safety of the ship and the sleeping crew rests in the hands of the crew members who are on duty, and this must never be forgotten. It is very easy as hour succeeds hour and nothing is seen and nothing happens, to lapse into a state of somnolence.

Danger in the shape of other vessels approaching on collision course, floating obstructions or a deterioration of the weather can occur in a surprisingly short time. It is vital that a constant lookout is kept at all times especially in the crowded waters around our shores. Never forget to look astern as well as looking in the more normal direction ahead. Because a yacht is so slow-moving, power driven ships have a nasty habit of coming up behind in an unexpected manner without being observed until dangerously close.

While on the subject of other vessels approaching your yacht we will consider the theory of collision courses. If two vessels sail on steady courses and if the bearing between them does not change then they will eventually collide (14). Conversely, if this bearing changes there will be no collision. How does one apply this theory in practice? A compass bearing should be taken of any vessel which might be on a collision course when it is first seen, and a little while later when it is nearer a second bearing is taken and compared with the first. Normally this produces different readings and all is well. The rate at which this bearing changes will increase as the vessel approaches the yacht. Otherwise, the position of the approaching vessel is noted against some suitable part of the yacht, say a stanchion, and provided the yacht is steered on a steady course and the observer does not move his position, a good estimate of any change of bearing can be made (15). If there is no danger of collision it will be seen to alter. It is important to understand and to practice this drill because your skipper will want early warning of the possibility of danger of collision so that he can be prepared to take evasive action. He will be furious, and rightly so, to be called on to deck to find danger imminent, but he will not be pleased to be called out of his warm bunk every time a ship comes over the horizon. However, if in doubt *always* call the skipper; he will not get his fair share of rest if he is worrying about what is going on on deck and wondering if the crew will call him in time.

The watch on deck have other duties to carry out. They have to keep the log book, check the yacht's equipment for wear and damage, trim and adjust the sails to get the best results, and above all else, steer the yacht.

Before dealing with steering a yacht at sea there are a few other things to mention and the first of these is noise. The deck of a yacht forms a sounding board and any bangs, bumps or heavy feet on deck, which may not be heard in open air, sound like someone beating a big drum when below. In addition any conversation held at normal levels in the cockpit can be easily heard below. Skippers resting in their bunks below often hear some home truths and sometimes get unexpected insights into their crews' characters. The crew on deck must always remember their mates off duty and resting below. The next point to remember is safety. Never forget that should you slip and fall over the side it is not easy for you to be picked up again, and the procedure for rescuing a man overboard that is discussed later in this book takes time. It therefore behoves the novice to be extra careful, and if he has to leave the safety of the cockpit in a seaway he should wear a safety harness. In any case move about the deck in a cat-like manner and never run—always remember the hand for yourself before the hand for the ship.

Helmsmanship

It is quite easy to learn to steer a yacht under good tuition, preferably in coastal waters where a sense of direction can be maintained by observing the coast. It is therefore advisable for novice helmsman to stand the first trick at the wheel or tiller in a cruise of this nature. Probably the best way to get the feel of steering is for the novice to hold the wheel or tiller in his hands while exerting no pressure. The instructor then places his hands on top of the novice's hands and steers the ship through his hands. A careful explanation of the effect of moving the wheel or tiller, coupled with demonstration, and the novice will be ready to steer the ship alone with suitable advice from his instructor, who must remain within reach of the wheel for some while until his pupil gains confidence. There are several tips to assist in good steering and these are well worth understanding.

A yacht is not like a car, because when the yacht's wheel is turned there is no immediate reaction. In a panic the novice will turn the

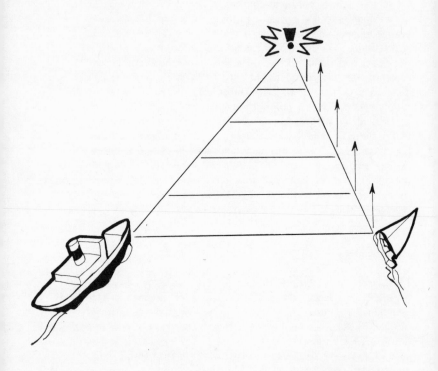

14 *If two vessels both stay on steady courses and speeds, and if the relative bearing between them does not change, they will collide*

15 *A rough way of checking if the relative bearing between another vessel and yours is changing is to steer a steady course and without moving your eye's position watch the approaching vessel lined up on some fixed object such as a stanchion. If it is seen to move, the relative bearing is changing*

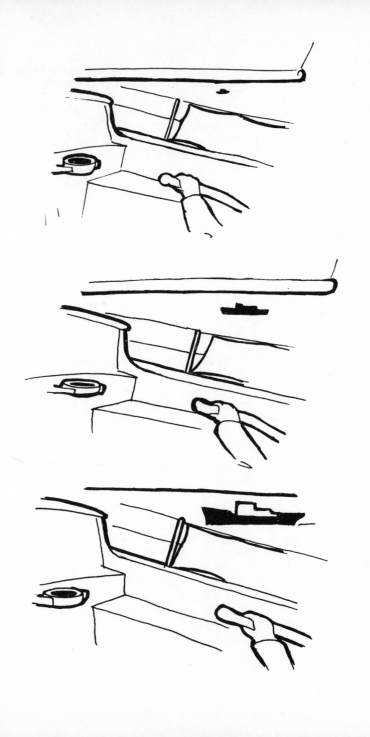

wheel still further and the yacht's head will swing past the desired course, so the novice again over-corrects in the opposite direction. The yacht swerves from side to side leaving behind a serpentine wake which is the signature of the learner helmsman. Remember that as a yacht weighs several tons and has considerable momentum the reaction to any alteration of the helm is slow and any alterations of direction must be made slowly by degrees. Results must not be expected at once. Also remember that, unlike a car, a yacht is steered from the stern and pivots about a point well aft of halfway. One of the best ways to see if the course is changing is to watch the yacht's bow move across the skyline ahead and then check against the compass, which is far better than watching only the compass to get immediate warning of a change of course. The compass card is damped to prevent undue swing in a seaway and therefore has a considerable time lag before it shows the change of course, which in turn lags behind movement of the rudder.

When sailing closehauled on the wind and beating to windward the ruling factor is how close to the wind you can steer while maintaining good boat speed. Every time the direction of the wind changes, and this is constantly happening, the direction in which the yacht is sailing is changed. The good helmsman will note by frequent reference to the compass the average course sailed and will pass it to the navigator or enter it in the log at the end of his trick (spell of duty) at the helm. The art of helmsmanship can only be learned by experience. A novice who has previously helmed sailing dinghies will find it quite easy to adapt himself to steering a yacht.

Steering a yacht efficiently to windward is largely a matter of co-ordinating information from all your senses, which with practice becomes almost second nature. You will feel the movement and speed of the hull through the waves, the heel of the boat, the strength and direction of the wind on your face, the pull on the tiller or wheel as the yacht tries to come head to wind. Your eyes will tell you the direction that the burgee is flying, if the sails are starting to lift near the mast, and the angle that the waves are making with the hull. With experience it is possible to tell by the feel of the yacht, even when below decks, if it is being sailed correctly.

When sailing off the wind the art is to steer a steady compass course without fighting the helm. Due to the effect of the waves the yacht will tend to wander from side to side of its true course and the helmsman's skill is to allow it the same deviation each side of the correct course in both time and amount so that the errors cancel out. At the same time he must apply only minor helm corrections so as not to slow down the boat. Watch out for the normal tendency to over-correct towards the windward side, especially if the wind is slightly aft of the beam, because the waves will cause the yacht to swerve more violently and farther in this direction.

When the wind is aft steering becomes hard work if there is any seaway running because the yacht tends to yaw (swerve) from side to side as each wave passes under the hull. In this case it will be necessary at times to fight the helm and apply large and powerful helm corrections to keep the yacht anywhere near the correct course. Skill in anticipating the corrections required will soon be acquired. The whole thing is a matter of constant repetition as each wave passing under the boat causes a similar series of swings from side to side. If the necessary corrections can be applied before the yaw occurs then less correction will be necessary and the boat will not be slowed as much as it would be by a violent correction after the yaw had commenced.

In general it can be said that a yacht has to be skilfully 'coaxed' to windward, 'allowed her head' off the wind, and 'fought' down-wind, but always remember that every helm correction slows down the boat and intelligent anticipation should be the aim.

Good steering requires considerable concentration and the rest of the crew on deck should remember this and not engage the helmsman in idle chatter or distract his attention in other ways. This is most important with the novice who has yet to learn to steer automatically. Also do not get in the helmsman's line of sight to the compass or the point on which he is steering, nor when adjusting sheets or similar manoeuvres push him around; after all, you would not treat the driver of a car in such a manner.

Using the compass

The beginner should understand the compass and how to use it for it is vital for navigation and steering. The normal yacht compass consists of one or more permanent magnets attached to a circular card or disc which is pivoted at its centre and is free to rotate in a bowl of fluid. The edge of the card is marked in 360° notation—in
D

any modern compass—and may have the points of the compass (NNE, NE, etc) included as well.

In the fore-and-aft line of the yacht on the edge of the bowl will be the lubber line against which the compass heading of the yacht is read. The first important thing to remember is that the compass card always remains stationary in relation to the earth (always pointing north) and the yacht with its lubber line moves around it as the yacht's heading is changed. Therefore, when steering a compass course the object is to move the lubber line around the compass card to the correct reading by using the helm. Remember that the fluid damps (reduces) and slows down any movement of the card.

When steering a compass course do not keep your gaze fixed on the card but get the vessel on the correct course, look up and select some suitable object on shore or horizon near some fixed part of the ship, say a shroud, and steer on that, checking every few seconds on the compass that the course is correct (16). This is most important at night, because helmsmen tend to get mesmerised by the compass and either go to sleep or steer very wild courses indeed, failing to keep a good lookout or watch the set of the sails (17). If the night is clear select some suitable star, but do not forget that the stars move across the sky as the night progresses, and a different one will have to be selected every so often.

Never put any iron object near the steering compass because it will make it give a false reading. Even a bunch of keys in an oilskin pocket or knives and forks in a washing-up bowl close to the compass will cause a deviation of several degrees, an electric torch, radio or another compass may cause even greater errors.

Some yachts are fitted with steering compasses of a type that can be used to take bearings on any object such as another ship by lining the object up with a rod in the centre of the card and taking the reading from the far side of the card. More frequently a separate hand-bearing compass will be used. In this case hold the hand-bearing compass away from you and sight the object concerned over the prism in which will be seen the compass card. When the object is in the V notch on top of the prism and the reading line is exactly under the V the correct bearing can be read. When taking bearings find a position such as the companionway where you can wedge the lower part of your body while leaving the upper part free to move around as the ship rolls. Also make sure that there are no metal objects where you are standing, such as rigging wires.

16   *When steering at night get the yacht on course and note if the moon or an easily recognized star is near some part of the mast or rigging. Use this as a steering guide, checking every few minutes that the compass course is correct*

17   *When steering a compass course by night do not get mesmerised by constantly staring at the card – look up and around every few minutes*

Always put the hand-bearing compass in its holder when not in use: it is easily damaged.

So far we have been talking about compass courses to steer and compass bearings from the ship to other objects. These are *compass* courses and bearings and this should always be stated when talking about them or noting them down. In addition the figures should always be repeated back by the recipient when one crew member is passing a course or bearing to another, as this avoids any possibility of error.

Streaming the log

The log is the means whereby the distance that the yacht has sailed through the water is measured, and it is normally a spiral rotator towed astern by a log line which in turn is connected to an instrument which measures the number of rotations and shows the result as nautical miles. The instrument is set in gimbals and mounted on the stern or quarter of the yacht. There are more modern electrical instruments that carry out the same function by making use of small propellers or probes which extend through the hull under water. The distance run and usually the actual speed is shown on dials. There are a number of these electrical instruments on the market, and as they are very simple to use and as each is different they are not considered here. The novice crewman must find out for himself or from other crew members how they work and if he has to take any action.

We will only consider the standard mechanical type of log and how to stream it and read it. First, always remember that the log rotator and the measuring instrument are expensive items of equipment, so treat them with care and make sure that they do not slip overboard. Unpack the log and put a few drops of oil in the oiling hole on the face of the instrument, set the hands on the two dials to zero, and note that one scale reads nautical miles from zero to nine, and the other reads from zero to 100 in tens. Sometimes there is a third dial reading tenths of a knot. Take the instrument aft to where there are special shoe plates on the rail which will receive the pins on the arm of the instrument, but before fixing it make sure that the lanyard is securely attached to a strong point nearby. Some yachts will have a shoe plate on each side of the hull; use the windward side for preference as the instrument is less likely to get dunked in the sea.

When the instrument is securely clamped to its shoe, collect the log line and log rotator. Take the hook end of the line and hook it to the eye at the aft end of the instrument. Stream the line in a bight (loop) over the side as you uncoil, until you are left with the log rotator in your hand and the log line streamed out astern and back to the instrument. Now throw the log rotator out to one side clear of the bight and the hull so that it does not foul itself.

The makers provide a table, usually to be found in the box, whereby the ship's speed can be calculated by counting the number of revolutions of the flywheel per minute. While on watch with nothing better to do it is a good idea to practice estimating the yacht's speed and checking it against the log.

Each hour and at various special times, such as when a tack is made, the log is read and the reading and time both noted in the log book. Care is necessary when the glass is speckled with water, as it is very easy to make a silly mistake especially at night and produce some quite impossible reading.

Handing the log

To hand (take in) the log grasp the log line about a foot astern of the instrument, pull in some slack and unhook it from the eye at the back of the instrument. Pull in some more line and feed the hook end through a fairlead or around a stanchion on the opposite side of the stern and back into the water. Now haul in the rest allowing it to run out through the fairlead as you do so until the rotator is in your hand and the whole line is streamed out astern the wrong way around. Finally pull it in, coil it and hang it up to dry. This procedure is necessary in order to get the twist out of the line; any attempt to coil it while the rotator is in the water will end with an impossible tangle. The instrument can now be unclamped from its plate, brought inboard and the lanyard untied. It should be dried, oiled and returned to its box.

It may be necessary to hand the log during the voyage. For instance, should you be becalmed the log and line will hang straight down and could become entangled with the propeller if the engine were started. Normally the log is handed just before entering port, and you can be helpful by reminding the skipper as this is easy to forget when dealing with the many other problems that occur at this time.

Heaving or casting the lead

Most modern yachts will be equipped with an electronic depth finder but will also carry a lead and lead line in case the electronic depth finder fails. A good crewman must know how to heave the lead and sound the depth in the simple traditional way.

The weight is usually a two-pound lump of lead with an eye at the top and a hollow in its base. This hollow can be armed (filled) with tallow so that when it touches the bottom it picks up a sample of the mud, sand, etc for identification. This is an advantage that a lead and line has over the electronic methods.

The line for a yacht is normally 20 fathoms long, traditionally marked as in Appendix G. Sometimes a simpler scheme for small yachts is used by marking each fathom with cord with knots in it up to five, i.e. one fathom one knot, two fathoms two knots and so until five fathoms; then from six to ten fathoms by two cords i.e. six fathoms with one knot in each, seven with two knots in each. Check to see what the code is on the line in your yacht. The method of heaving the lead, sounding and reporting the depth found is given in Appendix G.

Assisting the navigator

The arts of navigation will at first be beyond the beginner, but there are many ways in which he can assist. Probably the novice's greatest asset, if he is young, is a pair of good eyes. This attribute is an invaluable help to both skipper and navigator in that you are able to spot distant buoys, land, lights, etc beyond their range. A word of warning here: make sure that you have actually seen the item in question. When eyes are tired after a night at sea and the light is not good, eyes can play tricks and you will see non-existent land, lighthouses and buoys. Always look away and back again several times, making sure that the object has not changed between glances. When you sight a buoy, light or other mark just report them as such, with their characteristics, rather than attempting to identify them, as mistakes are easily made.

The use of the hand-bearing compass and log have already been mentioned, and some skippers will let you use these instruments. The log book is another thing that you may be able to help with. Usually there is a deck or rough log which has to be completed every hour and whenever anything special happens such as tacking or changing to another course. This book has ruled columns which may include compass course, log reading, wind strength and direction, state of weather and sea, barometric pressure, temperature of sea and air. Also included are sail changes, watch changes, any navigational marks seen and their characteristics and bearings. In fact everything is recorded that could be of use or information, together with the time of the event.

A separate form is used for recording weather forecasts and it is also most important that these should be correctly recorded. The novice can score a good point here if he reminds the skipper that a radio weather message is due. Most skippers, being very busy with other thoughts, tend to forget to switch the radio on in time!

A point here on accuracy; always be strictly honest about any course that you steer. If, for instance, you have made a mistake and have been steering a wrong course always tell the navigator exactly what you did, so that he can plot where you are actually going as opposed to where he thinks you are going. It is better to be honest than run onto a rock! The same applies if you have been unable to keep to a course because of a wind change. Tell him the course you really have been steering, and how long you have been on it.

Sailing at night

Preparations for night sailing must be made well before dark so that if some of the gear is faulty it can be corrected in daylight. All lights (spreader, masthead, navigation, compass and instruments) have to be checked to see that they are working. Salt water and electrics do not agree, and faults are sometimes found. Torches should be checked and put ready to hand, and an Aldis light or other bright signalling lamp connected up and tested, as this will be required if another vessel should come close during the night. White flares should also be to hand for the same reason.

The watch on deck should put on thick, heavy clothing as it gets very cold at sea directly the sun sets, even during the summer months. The cook should prepare food for the night watches and it is a good idea to provide a substantial meal that can be eaten before darkness falls.

Once it is dark even greater care must be taken when working on deck, as the chance of being picked up should you fall over the side is even more problematical. Some skippers insist that everyone leaving the cockpit at night must wear safety harness even in calm weather. It is essential to wear harness if there is a heavy sea running.

When first coming on deck after dark be very careful as you will not be adjusted to the dark, noise, wind and motion for some minutes, and you will not get your night sight for at least twenty minutes. Be very careful when you shine a torch or switch on cabin lights as bright light, even a match flame, will ruin night sight for a similar length of time. Remember that your eyes are not so sensitive in the centre of your vision, and in the dark you can see better if you do not look directly at the object that you want to see.

It is difficult to keep a sense of direction on a dark night at sea. The compass is a means of keeping direction but, as already mentioned, if gazed at continuously it will tend to mesmerise (17). However, there are often lighter patches of cloud, stars, shore lights, the loom of lighthouses over the horizon, or there may be some slow-moving boat showing navigation lights which can be used to assist in keeping a sense of direction, but be careful of moving lights close at hand. The feel of the wind on the face is an added aid to orientation.

The novice should have knowledge of the lights used by common vessels at sea so that when he is on watch he can assess what other vessels in his vicinity are doing and where they are going. Practice with a simple model at home will assist in understanding this problem. See Appendix H for the simplified collision rules, and details of some of the lights.

Seasickness

Seasickness hangs like a grim spectre over every yacht as it goes to sea as almost everyone succumbs at some time or other to this dreaded scourge. There are very, very few yachtsmen who are lucky enough to have cast iron stomachs and who are never sick even at sea in a gale. However, the majority of yachtsmen acquire their sea legs after a day or two and become more or less immune while they remain at sea. There are others who, after the first voyage of the season, never suffer for the rest of the year. It is advisable for the newcomer to yachting to work on the assumption that he is going to be one of those subject to seasickness, until proved to the contrary. In this way he will prepare himself in advance, obtain the necessary drugs, and will not be too shattered and disappointed if he does succumb.

Most experienced yachtsmen have their own ideas as to which things are conducive to seasickness and what will prevent it. Unfortunately they differ widely. The only agreed factors that will postpone the onset or prevent it altogether are as follows. First keep warm and dry: simple to say, but if you are feeling queasy it is difficult to force oneself below to get the correct gear. Perhaps someone who is feeling fit can be persuaded to go below and get your gear which you can put on on deck, or better still dress in adequate clothing well in advance. Secondly, do not go to sea on an empty stomach but munch some dry biscuits at the first sign of seasickness and keep on doing so every few minutes. Have a good supply of these biscuits or hard boiled sweets in your oilskin pockets before leaving port. Do not go below and work unless you are sure that you are immune, especially if you have to deal with something smelly such as the galley or the engine, because all smells tend to provoke seasickness. If possible get the skipper to give you some job on which you will have to concentrate and thereby forget your worries about seasickness.

It is surprising how quickly any nasty feeling will go away if you are not thinking about it. Try not to think too much about the problem and if other members of the crew are sick be sympathetic but make a mental note that you are at least one up on them, but do not crow too much as it may be your turn next!

There are other factors involved; fear is one, drinking and dining too well before going to sea is another. A hangover is a sure recipe for seasickness.

Several suitable anti-seasick drugs are available and can be bought at chemists, but their efficiency and side effects vary from person to person. All that can be advised is to try the different brands until you find one that suits your system. All of these drugs have to be taken in advance and many crew members take one the night before going to sea and another before setting sail. To take one when you are already feeling seasick is often too late and may soon bring on an attack. Crew who are seasick are naturally not as efficient as normally. In extreme cases efficiency can be reduced to dangerous levels.

Should you eventually succumb always be sick over the rail to leeward, and hold on tight as it is very easy to slip over in a heavy sea when oblivious to everything but your misery. Should someone else be sick when you are yourself well, keep a firm grip on their clothing to prevent this happening or help them into a safety harness, which must of course be clipped to some suitable place. Never ever be sick in the heads or down below and do not expect anyone to look after you if you are sick. Should you be sick over the deck, companionway, floor, etc you will be expected to clear up the mess yourself. Seasickness is such a common occurrence that it is treated as an everyday event. Crew members who are seasick are expected to carry out their normal duties and your good crew will be found to be doing his job as though nothing had happened. This takes a tremendous effort of willpower, especially if you have been sick for some time and your only wish is that the yacht would sink as quickly as possible. You decide that if you survive you will never under any circumstances go to sea again. However, when you have got over your attack you will soon forget all about it and will join the vast majority who have said the same thing many times over and who are still sailing and enjoying it! Determination to overcome seasickness is perhaps the best pill of all.

5 Sail Trimming and Changing

So far on our trip we have been sailing along without need to worry about the trim of the sails nor have we had to change them or even to tack on to another course. Let us consider them individually sail by sail. It will be appreciated that more than one sail may have to be dealt with at the same time when tacking and gybing, so a drill is necessary which may involve all crew members on deck. Those drills must be practiced in advance, especially with an inexperienced crew.

Mainsail

Trimming

Any adjustment to the mainsheet is usually very simple on a small yacht and provided the sheet is secured correctly on its cleat there should be no troubles.

In larger yachts a sheet winch may be used to get the sheet really tight when closehauled, or two or more crew members may have to sweat it down tight, one pulling down and the other taking in slack round the cleat. If a double ended mainsheet is used, it requires less effort to take in the windward end, as a better result can be obtained pulling the boom over. Other adjustments to get the best out of the main involve the use of the boom downhaul, kicking strop, clew outhaul, and sometimes a foreguy. In general one tries to have a flattish sail when closehauled and when the wind is strong, and a more curved shape when off the wind and if the wind is light.

45

Tacking

When going about from one tack to another, i.e. tacking, no action is necessary on the main except to avoid the boom and sheets as they swing across. The boom, being heavy, can give you a nasty crack. The first command (18) is 'Ready about', which gives the crew warning that they must be prepared for a tack. Sometimes the skipper will want a reply 'Ready' from crew members when they are ready to tack. This is followed by 'Helm's a'lee'. This indicates that the helm has been put over to bring the bows of the yacht through the wind onto the new course. Finally the cry 'Lee-oh' indicates that the yacht is head to wind and sheets and runners have to be taken in and let go. In lighter yachts the crew should move to the windward side of the cockpit and in yachts with running backstays they should take up the new windward stay and let off the new leeward stay as the boom comes across. When a trained crew is on deck the calls are normally reduced to just 'Lee-oh'. In some large yachts that are slow in stays (slow in going about) it may be necessary to have an additional order 'Let draw'—more about this under the heading Foresails.

Gybing

Gybing the main is something that requires care especially when in strong winds, and also when a yacht is equipped with running backstays. Before anything can be done, boom foreguys, if rigged, will have to be released. The best arrangement for gybing is to have a crew member in some secure and safe place aft where the flying sheets cannot hit him. His job is to take in the main sheet as fast as possible until the boom is close inboard; the helmsman meanwhile steers a steady course. The preparatory call (19) for this manoeuvre is 'Stand by to gybe', with the usual reply of 'Ready' from the crew. The executive call is 'Helm up', when the helmsman puts his helm over to bring the yacht onto the new course and the wind on the other quarter. As the boom swings across and to the cry of 'Gybe-oh' the two running backstays are made up and let go respectively. The man on the mainsheet pays out the sheets as fast as possible without burning his hands by letting them run out too fast. Care is necessary when gybing to

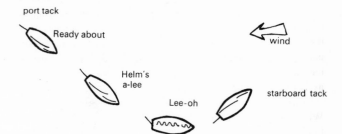

18   *When tacking, 'Ready about' means prepare to cast off or haul in sheets, runners, etc. 'Helm's a-lee' means the helm has been put over to bring the head to wind and onto the new course. 'Lee-oh' means that the vessel is head to wind and sheets and runners have to be taken in and let go. With experienced crews some or all of these calls are omitted*

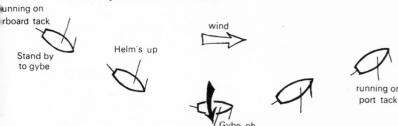

19   *When gybing, 'Stand by to gybe' is the warning call and 'Helm's up' the cry when the helm has been put over to bring the yacht onto the new course. As the boom swings over 'Gybe-oh' is the call. At this moment the mainsheets are pulled in and the runners adjusted*

avoid being hit by the boom as it swings across, or being caught up in the sheets, as they can hurt as they snap taut. The headsails can be left unattended (except a spinnaker) and can be trimmed after the main has been dealt with.

Reefing

If the wind becomes too strong for the amount of sail carried (size of sail) and the yacht is being pressed it will become necessary to reef. There are two methods of reefing a mainsail: roller reefing, in which the foot of the sail is rolled up like a blind by revolving the boom, and the older method of slab or tied down reefing where a whole section of the bottom part of the sail is tied down onto the boom. The first method is easier to carry out and is usually found on most modern yachts, but roller reefing may distort the shape of the sail so that it does not set as well as with a tied down reef.

Always before reefing put on oilskins and a safety harness. When reefing is necessary the sea may be rough and you will need both hands for the job. The drill for the roller type of reefing is as follows: put the reefing handles in position, cast off the kicking strap if fitted and stow, cast off the boom downhaul from its cleat and free the tackle so that the boom can rise to the top of its slide. In some yachts it will be necessary to take up the topping lift when reefing, and to keep the weight of the boom on the lift, while the sail remains reefed. Now lower away on the main halyard, keeping a half turn around its cleat, so that the boom is at the bottom of its slide, then wind it up to the top of the slide with the reefing gear. See that the luff rope comes off the mast together with any slides and winds down onto the boom clear of the reefing gear, and that the luff rope does not pile up on itself. It may be necessary to open a little gate on the mast track to let the slides come free. Care must also be taken to see that the leech winds on smoothly, and it may be necessary to have someone pulling the leech out along the boom as it is rolled up. It may be necessary to remove the lower batten from the sail. When the boom has been wound up to the top of its slide the same procedure as given above is followed until the required number of turns have been made and the sail is reduced to the right size for the strength of wind. Reefing handles are easily lost on the foredeck and must be stowed when not in use.

With tie or point reefing only two or sometimes three reductions of sail area are possible. These reductions are made where there is a line of reef points (short lengths of rope) across the sail with a cringle (reinforced hole) at each end of the row (66). To reef a sail in this manner it is preferable to get the boom into its gallows and lash it in place as this gives the crew something firm to hold on to, because trying to tie reef points with the boom free to swing from side to side is a difficult and dangerous task.

Having secured the boom lower away on the main halyard until the cringle on the luff (66) is just above the boom, lash this cringle to the mast end of the boom with a strong piece of rope, then lower the main halyard a bit more until the cringle on the leech is just above the boom and lash this fast with a rope around the boom and a few turns through the outhaul. When this is secure tie the opposite reef points together round the slack part of the sail that is to be reefed with (how did you guess?) a reef knot (70). Do not tie the points around the boom. Now unlash the boom from the gallows and take up any slack in the main halyard and the task is finished.

It is to be hoped that your skipper will not leave the reefing in a rising wind too long, as the stronger the wind and the rougher the sea becomes the more difficult is the task and the longer it takes to carry out.

Shaking out a reef is usually delightfully easy as there will be less wind and the sea should be calmer. The procedure to be adopted is exactly that of putting in a reef but in the reverse order. It will not be necessary to lash the boom to its gallows in shaking out a tied reef unless there is a heavy sea running at the time.

Headsails

Most yachts today have only one headsail, which is set on the jibstay (topmast forestay). This runs from the bow to the top of the mast. However, the procedure explained below is similar for yachts fitted with two headsails, a jib on the outer topmast stay (or jibstay) and a staysail on an inner stay (forestay). This will require two sets of halyards, sheets and winches, but has the advantage that the sails can be smaller and that any reduction in foresail area can be made very easily by downing one of the two sails.

One finds occasionally a foresail that is provided with the reefing points and cringles, but this is unusual. To reduce a foresail one exchanges it for a smaller sail made of a heavier material. The largest sail is the genoa, of which there may be several on board made of different weights and strengths of material. These may be labelled No. 1 or genoa, with some indication of its function, such as light weather genoa, etc.

The next in descending size is No. 2 and so on until No. 6 or thereabouts, which would be the smallest and is often referred to as the storm jib.

Changing

The drill for changing headsails is best carried out with a crew of two, but can of course be carried out by one man although taking much longer. The crew should be in oilskins and if there is any sea running or if it is at night safety harness should be worn. The new sail is got on deck, the bag lashed down, and the tack shackled on. It may be possible to get most of the hanks clipped on to the forestay under those of the existing sail, perhaps by casting off the bottom one or two to make space for those of the new sail. Cast off the foresail halyard falls and make sure that they are not tangled and will run freely. Do not forget to send the bag below, now the sail is out of it. Tell the helmsman, by sign preferably, that you are ready to down the foresail, when he can slow the yacht down by coming almost head to wind, which will help you to drop the sail on the deck. He can help further by freeing the sheets as the sail comes down. Directly the original sail is down unshackle the halyard from it and shackle it to the new sail, making sure that it does not get adrift or fouled. Do the same with the sheet, and check that the ropes have not got twisted in the process. Unhank the original sail from the forestay, and if dry put it in its bag, with the tack at the top, and stow below. If it is wet pass it down below for loose stowage. Hoist the new sail as soon as possible using the drill already explained.

Yachts equipped with twin headstays have a tremendous advantage in that the new sail can be prepared in advance, hoisted and trimmed before the original sail is lowered.

Trimming

Headsails are trimmed (adjusted to the wind) by using the winches in the cockpit to pull in the sheet. These winches usually turn in a clockwise direction and may be of the two or even three speed variety. Have a good look at them when you first join the ship and find out how they work, where their handles are stowed and the drill used. Normally one crew member turns the winch and another tails (pulls) on the end of the sheet as it comes off the winch barrel.

When the sheet has been pulled in the correct amount and the sail is correctly trimmed the crewman working the winch should grasp the rope around the barrel of the winch. This will stop it slipping back while his mate makes up the free end round a cleat. When the sheet has to be let off and it is still under load it can be surged (let off bit by bit) using the same technique of a hand grasping the rope around the winch barrel as its end is taken from the cleat. Take care that you do not get a riding turn (cross turn) which is caused by holding the free end of the sheet at the wrong angle. This can cause a jam which is difficult to clear. Riding turns can also occur if the lead to the winch is not at the correct angle, or if the sheet is slack and the sail flogging. Do not get your fingers caught between the sheets and the winch: the forces involved are considerable.

Take care of the winch handles and stow them properly. They are expensive items which easily slip overboard.

Tacking

When tacking from one closehauled tack to the other a cockpit drill is necessary if the manoeuvre is to be carried out efficiently. Each skipper will have his own variation of this drill and only an outline is given here. On the command 'Ready about' one crew member sees that the falls of the headsail sheet being used are not tangled and that the winch handle has been removed. He grips the rope round the winch barrel with one hand and undoes the sheet from its cleat with the other and then reports 'Ready'. On some yachts a hand may have to go up to the foredeck to make sure that a large sail such as a genoa does not foul the mast as it passes from one side to the other. The new sheet that is to be hauled in when the other is freed should have been prepared by the crew in the cockpit by hauling in any slack, placing one turn round the winch barrel and the handle ready to hand. The helmsman will then call 'Helm's a'lee' and the yacht starts to turn (18). Directly the wind ceases to fill the headsail the sheet that has been in use is freed and the opposite sheet is pulled in as fast as possible. If the helmsman holds the yacht a moment just past the head to wind position, before paying off, the new sheet can be pulled fully home and three more turns put round the barrel of the winch. The other cockpit hand then tails on the sheet as the first

E

puts the handle on the winch and winches in and finally cleats the sheet. The points to watch are: ensure that the old sheet pays out without jamming, that the new sheet is only pulled in when free of obstruction, that at least three turns must be put round the winch before the *full* weight of the wind comes on the sail. It will at once be apparent how necessary it is to have a practised drill for this manoeuvre, with each of the crew working as a member of a team.

A modern yacht when closehauled sets the genoa inside the rail and the lead of the sheet has to be changed when sailing off the wind. It may also be necessary to move the position of the sheet block and tack to get a better shape in the sail. This block is usually mounted on a slide so it can be moved quickly.

Do not forget to enter the details of a sail change, tack, etc. in the deck log, together with details of the log reading and time and any other information.

Backing

Some yachts are difficult to tack in heavy seas because they will not carry their way past the head to wind position and either fall back onto their original tack or start to go astern. The yacht is then said to be in stays. In this case, instead of freeing the headsail sheet when it ceases to draw, the original sheet is still held taut. The wind will then blow on the back of the headsail and drive the head of the yacht around. When the bow is safely past the head to wind position the skipper orders 'Let draw' and the original sheet is freed and the leeward one winched in.

Heaving to

When it is desired to stop a yacht at sea in order, say, to cook a meal in rough weather or to allow the crew to rest, it is 'Hove to'. To do this the headsail is backed by going about as explained above or by sheeting it across to the opposite side. At some position of the tiller the yacht will settle down and quietly jog along unattended with the tiller lashed (20).

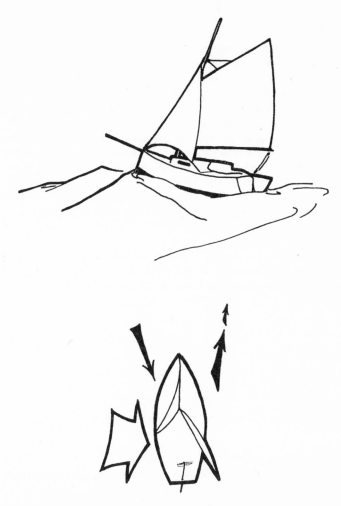

20 *A sailing yacht is hove-to by having the headsail sheet pulled over to the windward side of the vessel. The headsail then tends to push the vessel astern or off the wind and counteracts the forward drive of the mainsail. It will be necessary to adjust the helm and to lash it in position to balance the drive forward against this pressure. The vessel is then nearly stopped*

Spinnaker

There are many skippers who will never use a spinnaker when cruising even in ideal weather. To be honest, 'playing' with spinnakers in light to moderate winds can be fun, and gives the crew something of interest to do. However in strong winds and rough seas spinnakers can be an expensive menace and they should only be used under these conditions when racing.

A spinnaker is a symmetrical triangular sail (69) the hoist (top) of which is attached to a halyard which leads to the very top of the mast. One corner of the foot is attached to the outer end of the spinnaker boom, which is put out on the side opposite to the main boom. This corner becomes the tack. The other corner becomes the clew and has a sheet to a block at the stern (22). This sail is normally only used when the wind is aft of the beam.

The correct stowage of a spinnaker in its sail bag is most important (21). It should be stowed so that the three corners are lashed to the mouth of the bag so that they cannot get twisted, and the body of the sail in the bag must be stowed with the two long sides edge to edge. As the sail is of light nylon this is not difficult.

Hoisting

The spinnaker in its bag is lashed to the pulpit with the hoist forward and the two corners to each side (21). The halyard (check to see that it is not twisted around the stay) is attached to the hoist of the spinnaker and a sheet rove from the leeward block on the stern to the leeward clew (the corner not on the boom). A similar rope is rove from the windward block on the stern to the tack on the windward side, but it is called a guy as it will also go to the end of the spinnaker boom. The ends of these two ropes—the sheet and the guy—go to the cockpit via blocks on each side of the stern, and are made fast to cleats or winches, depending on the size of the yacht. Two lighter lines (foreguys) are attached to the tack and clew of the spinnaker and lead through blocks in the very bow of the yacht to act as a downhaul for the boom (22).

The spinnaker boom is now rigged on the windward side of the yacht. It clips onto a fitting on the forward side of the mast; the other end is clipped to the windward clew of the spinnaker which is also on the end of the guy. A topping lift is usually attached to the top of the spinnaker boom and it is now topped up to clear the rail and pulpit before the sail is hoisted.

To hoist the spinnaker one crew hauls away on the halyard, carefully watching the sail (not his hands) to see that it does not catch anything. Another, if available, guides the sail out of its bag keeping the two edges together to prevent it filling with wind prematurely and a third manages the sheet and guy in the cockpit (23).

When the sail is almost hoisted the guy can be gently adjusted so that the boom is almost 90° to the wind and the sheet gently pulled in so that the sail is drawing. When fully hoisted and cleated the foredeck hand slides the spinnaker boom up the mast as high as necessary to suit the strength and direction of the wind and adjusts the topping lift and downhaul so that it is at 90° to the mast and the foot of the sail is parallel to the deck.

Any other headsail that is still set may be lowered and securely lashed to the rail, or removed and stowed below. Sometimes a special foresail is set inside the spinnaker to obtain extra drive.

Trimming

In most conditions it is necessary to trim the spinnaker by adjusting the sheet, guy ropes and boom position at very frequent intervals in order to keep it drawing correctly. As the sheet is let out so the guy is pulled in and vice versa. Letting out the guy tends to fill the sail as the boom goes forward, but the sail draws best when it is only just full. The art of trimming a spinnaker for maximum results will be obtained with practice.

Gybing

There are three main ways of gybing a spinnaker and the choice of these rather depends on the type of gear and the skipper's preference. If the yacht has a single spinnaker boom which is of a length that will pass inside the forestay when its heel is slid up the mast, then the dipping boom method is used (24). All that is necessary is for the outer end of the boom to be unclipped from the spinnaker

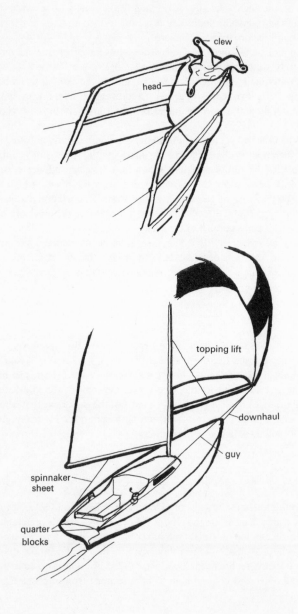

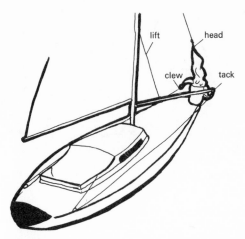

lift | head | clew | tack

21 A spinnaker must be stowed in its bag with its three corners lashed at the top and the sail not twisted. It is normally fed into the bag head first, with the edges together. Before hoisting the bag is secured to the pulpit

22 A spinnaker boom is rigged on the windward side of the yacht, one end clipped on or in a socket on the foreside of the mast and the other end clipped to the tack of the spinnaker. A topping lift and downhaul are also attached to this boom. A boom guy is connected to the tack of the spinnaker and a sheet to the clew. A halyard is attached to the head

23 The spinnaker is hoisted and the boom trimmed so that it is at approximately 90° to both the wind and mast. The height of the boom and the length of the sheet are then adjusted to give the most efficient sail shape

and guy, leaving the guy attached to the sail so that it then becomes a sheet. The end of the boom is dipped under the forestay and clipped to the other corner of the sail. Most booms have a special remote controlled clip that can be opened by pulling on a light line running the length of the boom.

A variation of this drill, if the boom is too long for the dipping method, is for it to be first removed from the mast so that it can be brought around behind the forestay before replacing on the mast and clipping to the sail on the opposite side.

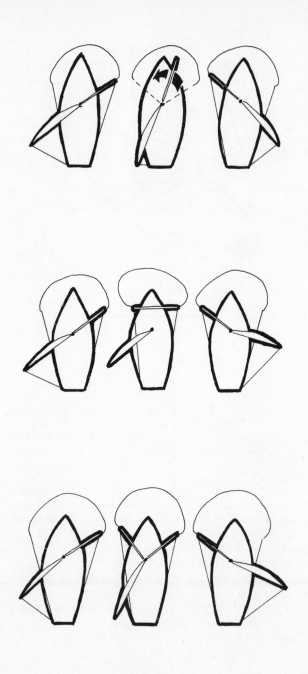

The next method is used with a double ended boom (25). The boom ends will both go into the sockets or rings on the mast and have clips to hold the sail and lines. The drill in this case is for the boom to be taken off the mast and clipped to the other side of the sail. At this time the boom will connect the two corners of the sail and there will be two guys. The boom is then pushed across the boat and the new lee end released from the sail and connected to the mast socket.

The third method involves two spinnaker booms (26). The second boom is rigged in the same way as the first but on the opposite (lee) side of the yacht. When it has been attached to the sail the original boom is unclipped from the sail and brought inboard and lashed down on deck.

When the spinnaker gybe has been completed the yacht and the main are gybed. The sails naturally will have to be re-trimmed for the fresh course.

Lowering

It is preferable to lower a spinnaker with the wind well astern as the main will help to smother the sail. If the spinnaker is to be replaced

24 *When gybing the spinnaker with the 'dipping boom' method, first slide the heel of the boom up the mast, then unclip the outer end from the tack of the spinnaker and swing it down behind the forestay to the leeward side, clipping it to the other corner of the spinnaker. Finally slide the heel of the boom down again and trim the sail*

25 *Gybing the spinnaker with the 'end to end' method, first detach the heel of the boom from the mast and attach it to the clew of the spinnaker (the boom is now attached to the two bottom corners of the sail), then detach the boom from the old tack and clip it into the socket on the mast, finally trimming the sail on its new gybe. This method is only possible with spinnaker booms that have clip fittings at both ends*

26 *Gybing the spinnaker with the 'two boom' method, first set up the second boom on the leeward side and attach this to the clew of the spinnaker, then detach the first boom from the sail and mast and stow it. Trim the sail on its new gybe*

27 *To lower the spinnaker first allow the spinnaker boom to go as far forward as possible. The sail is then lowered under control while being collected under the main boom and fed down the companionway hatch. It is then detached from its boom, sheet and guy and re-bagged. The boom is lowered and stowed*

with another headsail this is first hoisted and trimmed inside the spinnaker (27).

The halyard falls are prepared so that it can be paid out without any fouls or snags developing. The spinnaker boom is then allowed to go well forward. When all this is ready the cockpit hand uncleats the sheet and takes it to the main companionway hatch. The foredeck hand unclips the tack from the boom as the sail is lowered and collected under the main boom, by catching the foot of the spinnaker and pulling it inboard, down the main hatch and into the saloon (27). The crew member on the halyard must watch carefully to see that he does not lower so fast that the sail falls into the water. When fully lowered it is unclipped from the guy and the sheet and halyard unshackled. The boom is then unshipped and lashed to its chocks on deck. All the rest of the gear must be coiled up and stowed.

Preparation

If the spinnaker is to be used again it has to be rebagged ready to hoist (21). This is normally done below as it is a light sail and in any wind is difficult to bag on deck. Sometimes used is an alternative method of preparation of putting the sail in stops (28). In this case the hoist (top) of the spinnaker is lashed to some strong point, and

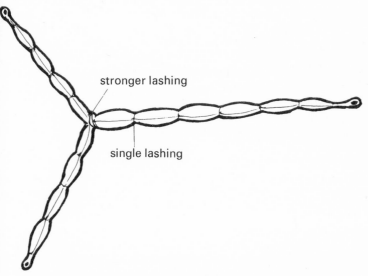

stronger lashing

single lashing

28   *To stop a spinnaker stretch it out tight, then working from the head bundle it edge to edge and lash it every 3 to 4 ft with single turns of 'rotton cotton' (thin, easily broken yarn). Repeat the process from the two bottom corners so that it forms a Y. At the junction make several extra turns with the cotton. The sail can now be hoisted and broken out when required. This procedure can be carried out with other headsails if required*

while the edges are kept together the sail is pulled tight. The body of it is bundled together and every metre a single tie of rotten cotton (a special type of cotton which easily breaks) is made. It is important that the sail is kept taut while this is being done. When the two corners are almost reached a stronger tie of several turns of the cotton is made. Next the two corners at the foot are secured and a similar procedure is followed working back from the two corners, but in this case the long edge of the sail and its foot are brought edge to edge. When the whole sail is stopped it looks like the letter Y.

Spinnaker wraps

Spinnakers have a nasty habit of getting twisted around the forestay if the wind is light and there is a sea running. Such a spinnaker wrap can be avoided by the use of a special net which is hoisted on the forestay in the same manner as a foresail. Sometimes a small special headsail which fills the gap between the bottom of the spinnaker and the deck is used to give extra speed. This is called a spinnaker staysail, and to a certain extent it can reduce the chances of a wrap. Another method is to attach a spare halyard to the samson post or other strong point on the foredeck as an inner forestay.

6 Emergencies

Gale

Gales are something to be avoided in a small yacht as they can be most unpleasant for the crew. The skipper should not put to sea if there is a gale warning for the sea area that you are in. Unfortunately, due to our quickly changing weather pattern it is sometimes possible to be caught some distance from land by a gale arriving without warning. While at sea in unsettled weather it is obvious that a constant listening watch should be kept on the radio for any gale warnings, as the earlier these warnings are received the greater the chance the skipper has of getting the yacht into some suitable port before it arrives to make life miserable. In addition it is most important to get the full details of the various weather broadcasts correctly recorded as they are received, so the skipper has the best data available on which to base his decision.

When caught out in a gale for the first time the continual noise of wind screeching through the rigging is very frightening and exhausting. The violent movement of the boat and the apparently huge waves also tend to unnerve crew experiencing their first gale.

The most important thing to remember is that providing the yacht is sound and you are a good way out to sea you are quite safe. The only danger is if you are approaching a lee shore (a shore onto which the wind is blowing), when every effort must be made to get away and out to sea where safety lies.

Providing that you are out to sea with a good stretch of sea room to leeward, the best plan is to ride out the gale under shortened sail, keeping one crew on watch while the others remain down below resting as best they may.

Under gale conditions any crew on deck should always wear safety harness. It is advisable to get into the harness while below and to clip the line on to a secure point before leaving the shelter of the hatch when going on deck. Those on deck should, of course, wear oilskins as there will be plenty of water flying around.

Naturally when the gale warning is received or the wind pipes up the skipper will make some preparations. Any gear on deck will be stowed below if possible and any which has to be left there will be doubly lashed down. All loose gear below must be securely stowed in safe places and equipment such as storm sails and safety harnesses put to hand. Bear in mind that the yacht may at times lie over on her beam ends (right over on her side) and stow gear accordingly.

As the wind increases so the sail area will be reduced by reefing the main and hoisting successively smaller headsails until the yacht is sailing under a storm jib and a fully reefed main. If further reduction is necessary the main can be lowered completely or exchanged for a trysail (Appendix B, 68). This is a special very small mainsail made of heavy material, with a pair of sheets attached to its clew (bottom aft corner). It is not attached to the boom and is called loose footed. When the mainsail has been lowered and the boom lashed to its gallows or crutch the mainsail slides are taken out of the mast track and the whole sail securely lashed to the boom with double ties. The trysail slides are then inserted into the mast track and the main halyard attached to the hoist (head). The trysail sheets are attached to the clew and thence to blocks on each side of the stern and then led back into the cockpit. The trysail is hoisted in a similar way to the main, but as it is very much smaller and does not have a boom the running backstays and topping lifts can be left up. Once hoisted the appropriate sheet can be taken in. It will usually be necessary to take this sheet to a free winch unless the sheets consist of tackles (68).

Should the wind get up still further it may be necessary to lower the trysail and even the storm jib and carry on under bare poles. It is surprising how fast a yacht will sail under bare poles, the mast, rigging, superstructure and hull acting as a sail. Sometimes when sailing this way and downwind the speed may be too great and the skipper may order warps to be trailed astern in long bights (loops)

64

from the stern cleats. Take care rigging these as the pull on these warps can be fierce.

By now most crew will have been sick. They may also be exhausted and soaking wet. They will be bemused by the noise and violence of the wind and sea. This state can be dangerous as wrong decisions are easily made, inadequate lookout kept and insufficient care taken when carrying out various tasks. It is now that the good crewman can really prove his worth in the fight, and fight it is, to keep the yacht in a proper state both on deck and below. It is all too easy to curl up in a bunk in an abyss of misery while sails flog themselves to bits on deck and the cabin floor is covered with a wet and dirty pile of assorted clothing and gear.

It is to be hoped that no reader of this book will ever find himself in a situation which can be classed as an emergency, but should the unexpected occur the ideas given below will be of vital assistance.

There are certain principles common to all such situations. Know where all safety gear is stowed and exactly how to work it. This applies to life-saving equipment such as liferafts, lifebuoys, lifejackets, safety harness, etc. and to warning signals, flares, lights, flags, smoke signals, radio, etc. The first aid equipment should not be forgotten. This is most important as it could be that you are the only person able to use them, and you could find yourself in the position of being skipper.

There is bound to be a great deal of noise and turmoil when disaster strikes, and it is here that a calm crewman with a steady nerve will be invaluable. It is often a good thing when idling away a watch to run through in your mind various disasters that could strike and to work out several contingent plans.

If disaster strikes suddenly and you are below decks, get out at once irrespective of dress, etc. Any warning that the crew on deck can give in the form of an 'All hands on deck' shout may save lives. If disaster gives adequate warning then careful plans can be made and preparation undertaken.

The more clothes worn the better, as they help to keep the body warm even in the water and supply extra buoyancy at the same time. The lucky possessor of a sub-aqua wet suit should wear it without fail. Heavy seaboots or yachting shoes should be discarded unless one expects to be washed up on a rocky coast.

Finally, though not the responsibility of the crew, it would be worth checking that there is someone ashore who knows what the skipper's plans are and who will raise the alarm if the yacht is overdue so that the search and rescue organisations can be alerted. HM Coast Guard have a '66—Passage Report Form' which can be used for this purpose.

Sinking at sea

Run down by another vessel

Provided that a good lookout is kept this should not occur, but in recent years there have been a number of incidents of yachts being run down by merchant and fishing vessels. Yachts hit by large steel vessels sink in a matter of seconds and when the threat is apparent all hands must be got on deck and lifejackets donned. The liferaft must be prepared for launching. There will be little time for any other action than to try to attract the attention of the lookout on the larger vessel by means of lights, flares, smoke, etc. A powerful torch or Aldis flashed at the bridge of the larger vessel may help, or shine a light on your mainsail.

Striking a submerged object

It is amazing the amount of junk that is to be found floating on or just under the surface of the sea. Some of this is so large that it may hole a yacht which strikes it. The hole is not likely to be large and the yacht will not sink swiftly. It may even be possible to staunch the flow of water by stuffing the hole with soft materials and padding it so that the bilge pumps, assisted by buckets, will enable the yacht to keep afloat (29). A better repair can then be made by nailing boards across the padding, or in a GRP yacht by bracing the boards in position. If possible a sheet of material (sail, awning) fothered (spread) over the hole on the outside of the hull will further reduce the flow (30). If the damage is in some place that cannot be got at, or the damage is so severe that the yacht may sink, all preparations to abandon ship must be made at the same time as temporary repairs are being put in hand.

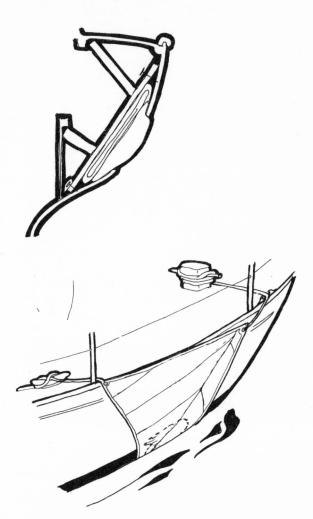

29 *Temporary repairs to a hole in the hull can be made by wedging pillows, mattresses, etc into the hole with floor boards across them, and held in place by jamming other lengths of timber against strong points*

30 *A sail fothered (spread) over the outside of a hole in the hull of a vessel and lashed in place will reduce the inflow of water considerably*

Failure of the hull or fittings

The hull of a yacht kept in good condition and regularly surveyed should not fail, but yachts which have not been cared for have been known to drop their keels and capsize. A major failure of the fabric of the hull or the skin fittings has occurred in some yachts in poor condition. Sometimes the leak is a small one and temporary repairs can be made which will enable the yacht to carry on, but in the event of a major failure the yacht may well sink.

Fire and explosion

Perhaps the greatest danger at sea is from fire and explosion, and care must be taken to see that there are no gas or petrol leaks and that any such leaks are quickly spotted and rectified. Gas should always be turned off at the cylinder valve when not in use. Should fire occur immediate action should be taken to extinguish it before it has got a hold and for this purpose several modern and effective fire extinguishers are required. If the numbers are sufficient part of the crew should fight the fire while the rest prepare rafts, etc. for abandoning ship.

The first aid kit, which should contain burn dressings, must be taken as it is likely that some of the crew may be burnt. Minor fires such as a pan of fat catching fire or a paraffin cooker flaring up should be dealt with with care and common sense. Panic reaction is very dangerous in a yacht. In the event of any fuel or gas being transferred it is mandatory that there should be no exposed flame or cigarettes alight at the time or afterwards until all trace of smell has disappeared.

Petrol and paraffin fires are best put out with fire extinguishers or sand; water must never be used. Burning fat can be put out by smothering the pan with a towel or blanket and again water must not be used. Water should only be used on burning materials such as wood, blankets, clothing, etc. Wet blankets or towels are invaluable for smothering fires and protecting the crew fighting them.

It may be necessary to run before the wind to enable the crew to fight the fire from the cockpit, but keep air away from the flames as much as possible.

Going aground

Striking isolated rocks in deep water

On some coasts there are outlying rocks which are located a long way from the land itself. If a yacht strikes one of these rocks the crew will find itself in the same predicament as if they were run down by another vessel, except that there is no possibility of immediate rescue from the vessel concerned. In addition to the immediate preparations for abandoning ship efforts will have to be made to get the yacht afloat again and if possible to effect temporary repairs in the manner as described above (29, 30). The great difference from being run down is that it is probable that waves will be breaking over the yacht and it may be pounding on the rocks. There is a real danger of being swept overboard under these conditions and there will be a loss of effective command due to the noise. Distress signals should be made which may be seen by watchers on the shore or more likely by other vessels near by.

Running aground on a rocky coast

Again, immediate preparation must be made to abandon ship while trying to refloat her and effect temporary repairs (29, 30). If the coast is steep-to and rocky it may be necessary on abandoning ship to try to find a better place to land further along the coast. This would, of course, depend on how rough it is and on the wind strength and direction. It may be better to try to land on a near-vertical face than to be washed by breaking waves up a gully between the rocks.

Clothing and shoes should be kept on to lessen damage to the body. If possible distress signals should be used. It is more than likely that waves will be breaking over the yacht and she will be pounding against rocks. There have been occasions when a yacht has been washed so far up the rocks that the crew have been able to scramble ashore, but this is unlikely.

Running aground on sand or mud banks

If there is a sea running at the time and the yacht grounds the drill will be similar to that above. If possible an anchor should be

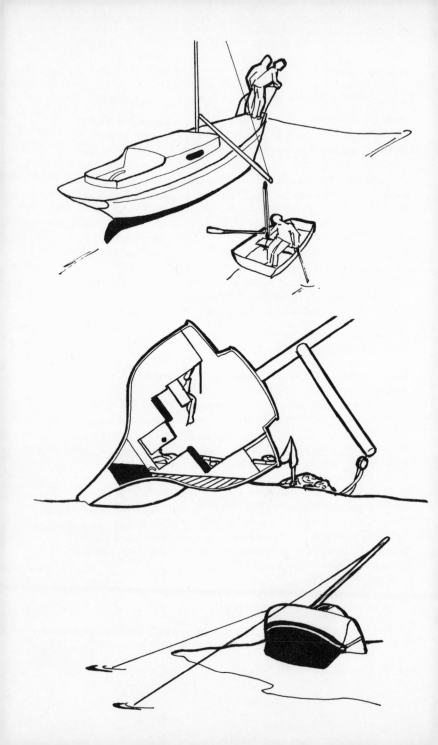

dropped to prevent the yacht being driven by the wind and waves further ashore. There is very little that can be done to refloat a yacht in heavy seas. The best hope is that the tide is rising and that the anchor will hold so that she may be pulled off before she breaks up. If the yacht goes aground in sheltered or calm conditions a great deal can be done to get her afloat again. When the tide is rising it is necessary to take the kedge anchor out to deep water in the dinghy so that when she floats she can be pulled off. If the tide is falling immediate action is necessary to heel the yacht over so that she draws less water. This can be done by making use of the sails; by standing off the boom with several crew members astride it; by having the whole crew forward to lift the stern; or by connecting the lower block of the main sheet to a dinghy in the water (31). At the same time a kedge must be put out into deep water so that the heeled yacht can be hauled off.

Should all this fail and it becomes obvious that the yacht will dry out, the necessary preparations should be made. If legs are available it may be possible to use them to stay vertical. If not, the yacht should be heeled over onto the side higher up the bank, usually towards the land. All gear likely to break loose must be secured and the effect that lying over will have on fuel, water and battery electrolytes considered. The bilgewater will ride up the inside of the yacht and may fill lockers from the back, so some may have to be emptied of gear. Locker doors on the upper side may burst open if the catches are not strong (32). When the tide has gone it may be

31   *Every effort must be made to heel the yacht quickly if she goes aground on a falling tide so that the draft will be reduced and she can get clear. The crew out on the main boom, or a dinghy bearing down on the end of the mainsheet tackle may do the trick. The crew on the foredeck may lift the keel clear if the deepest draft is aft*

32   *A yacht that goes aground and dries out will lie over on her side at a considerable angle. When this occurs bilgewater may run up behind lockers, tanks and vents may leak, doors and lockers burst open and gear slip overboard*

33   *When a yacht is high and dry it will be possible to resite the anchor in the best position to pull her off when the tide rises. A kedge anchor can also be put out on the end of the main halyard to help pull the yacht up at the vital time when the water reaches the cockpit coamings*

possible to resite the kedge and also attach another anchor to the main halyard to assist in righting the yacht when the tide turns (33).

Man overboard

Several times we have mentioned the problem of a crew member falling overboard and have pointed out that there is a considerable risk involved in that not only will it take time to pick up the person concerned, but there is a chance that it may not even be possible to find him, especially at night and in rough weather.

Some skippers will not only have a special 'man overboard' drill prepared but will insist that it is practised at the start of a cruise, using some floating object such as a fender or lump of wood in place of a body.

There are several acceptable drills (34) the choice of which depends on the type and size of yacht, its rig at sea, size of crew and the skipper's personal preference. There are two basic drills, the gybe-round-at-once (traditional) drill and the sail-straight-on drill, leaving a trail of flotsam until all crew are on deck when a reciprocal course is sailed. There are several common points. First, the remaining crew on deck must at once yell 'All hands on deck' at the top of his voice directly anyone falls overboard. This call must *only* be used in dire emergency and all crew must realise that they must get on deck as they are, dressed or undressed, directly they hear the cry. Some yachts use a whistle instead of a call as it will cut through the noise of the wind. This call or whistle is also used when other emergencies occur such as when there is imminent danger of being run down. Secondly, the crew on deck must throw a lifebuoy to the man in the water in the shortest possible time. This may be attached to a Dan buoy (a float with a tall pole and flag). If the yacht is moving fast this will land some way from him unless it is thrown promptly. Thirdly, the next available crew member on deck must get to a vantage point and point at the man in the water and never take his eyes off him. This is most important as the skipper and the rest of the crew rushing on deck will be severely disoriented and some vital decisions have to be taken which have to be right first time if the man in the water is to be recovered.

Here the two methods and drills divide; the 'gybe-round' school

34 *In the 'gybe around' method of picking up a man overboard,
the helm is put hard over at once (in the case of tiller steering
the helm up to windward) and the yacht gybes to make a circle,
returning to a position close to where the man fell overboard*

*When there is a strong wind or when the boom has a foreguy
rigged it is advisable to use the 'carry on' method of picking up
a man overboard. While the rest of the crew are coming up on
deck keep on a steady course throwing floating objects such as
cushions over the side at regular intervals. Directly all is prepared sail
back along the reciprocal (180° difference) course, checking your
position by the trail of cushions, etc to the point where the man was
lost*

will gybe all standing and all being well will be in a position to pick up the man in the water (34). The 'carry-on school' will proceed to leave a trail of any floating material, cushions, fenders, reserve lifebuoys, the more colourful the better. Meanwhile the helmsman will be steering his original course with great care and noting the time and speed. The skipper with the rest of the crew, but excluding the pointer and the helmsman, will prepare the yacht so that it can be sailed back down a reciprocal course for the same distance it has traversed since the man fell overboard (34).

Without getting too involved with the respective advantages and disadvantages of the two schools of thought, it would be usual to use the first method in a small cruiser in normal weather if the boom did not have a foreguy (preventer) rigged, and the second method would be used by a large yacht or ocean racer or any yacht in heavy weather when it would be impossible or dangerous to gybe all standing (without taking in the sheets).

At night the procedure is similar, but a lighted Dan buoy or flare must be put over the side at the same time as the lifebuoy. In most yachts this is tied to the lifebuoy so that it goes over automatically with it. Some yachts will be equipped with a number of little light floats that can be thrown over to mark the route back. The Aldis lamp should be on deck but should be used with care so as not to blind other crew members.

Having got back to the man in the water, it is a difficult task to get him back on board because he will be exhausted and water-logged, and due to the height of the rail above the water it is difficult to reach down to him and catch him, let alone haul him on board. There are a number of ideas that could be adopted depending upon the circumstances. Ropes can be trailed over the side in bights (loops) secured at each end (but be careful of fouling the propeller); a sail can be lowered, usually the jib, and allowed to hang over the rail (36); a boarding ladder can be rigged if it is not too rough; motor tyre fenders can be hung at water level; and a strong crew member can go overboard on a safety harness to pass a line around him if he is tiring or a casualty. Any other spare crew should lie on the deck alongside the rail and may be able to grab him as the yacht sails past. Remember it is not easy to bring a yacht to a standstill at an exact place in the water.

It is impossible in a book of this nature to deal with every action necessary in emergencies. Such obvious actions as lowering the sails, starting the engine, using the radio (if available) and selecting the most important items to take when abandoning ship have not been mentioned. These will to a large extent depend on the situation at the time.

The reader should not think that because this section on emergencies has been included that they are frequent events. Happily they are very rare indeed.

7 Arrival in Harbour

At long last, after all our experiences, the foreign coast is sighted and expectations of calmer waters, peace and quiet are uppermost in the minds of most crew members. If the visibility is good and the land high do not be surprised to find it may take four or five hours before you have reached the harbour. It is possible to see high land many miles out to sea in good conditions.

When the harbour is approached be very careful not to irritate the skipper with constant questions and idle chatter. From his point of view this is the period most fraught with tricky decisions upon which the safety of the yacht depends, and anything that will distract him is very unwelcome. Do not under any circumstances stand up on the foredeck or deck in front of him; after all the driver of a car would be very annoyed if you sat on the bonnet of his car when he was driving through traffic. Also keep clear of the chart table and the companionway as the skipper will be popping up and down like a jack-in-a-box checking what he can see against the chart, unless he is familiar with the port you are entering.

Preparation

While still out at sea some preparation has to be carried out and gear put to hand. Usually the boathook will be unlashed and fenders, lines and heaving line brought up on deck. The fenders should be tied to some secure point to prevent them falling overboard. The sail ties are passed one turn round the boom or tied to a handy point. Bow or stern lines should have a large loop tied

76

with a bowline in the end on top of the coil, which is lead out through the fairlead and back over the rail ready to hand. The other end of the coil is secured to the cleat and back under through the fairlead to a cleat or post. Thus the free end can be pulled away without a tangle developing (46). The heaving line is coiled ready for throwing and placed in some handy secure place such as the cockpit, together with several spare lines.

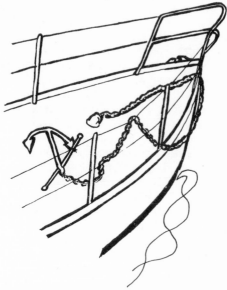

35 *The anchor is prepared for dropping by leading the cable through the bow fairlead and back over the rail to the anchor so that it may be picked up and dropped overboard without a snarl-up or delay*

The anchor is unlashed and the cable led from the navel pipe through the bow fairlead and back over the rail and to the anchor shackle so that the anchor can be picked up and dropped over the rail at short notice with no chance of a snarl (35). Some skippers like to have a length of cable flaked along the deck, usually about five fathoms, if there is any chance of the cable jamming as it comes up through the navel pipe from the anchor locker. An alternative method of preparing an anchor for dropping is to hang it over the bow clear of the water on a very short scope of chain, sometimes referred to as 'hanging off the anchor'. The chain must be secured by passing round a samson post, a winch with the brake on, or through a cable stopper, ready to be slipped at the right moment. On some yachts it may be possible to place the stock of the anchor in the anchor fairlead with the crown sticking out over the bows. In this case it is only necessary to slip the chain and to give the anchor a push to overbalance it when it is required to drop it. This method should not be used when there is any seaway running because the anchor may damage the paintwork as it swings about.

Depending on the type of dinghy carried and on the skipper's plans it may be unlashed, prepared and launched prior to reaching the harbour. It is often an advantage to have a dinghy already in the water when entering harbour. The log will have to be handed.

If it is a foreign country you are visiting the skipper will order the courtesy ensign of the country concerned to be flown from the starboard signal hoist. This is normally found running to a block on the crosstrees (spreaders). The Q signal flag (plain yellow) is hoisted in the same way from the port signal halyard. These flags will have a wooden toggle at their hoist which slips into a loop on the halyard. The flags will also have a loop at their foot into which a toggle on the bottom half of the halyard fits. These flags should be hoisted when inside the three mile limit. The Q flag indicates that all aboard the yacht are healthy and Pratique (Customs clearance, etc.) is requested. When this has been obtained the Q flag is lowered but the courtesy ensign is kept flying by day while in that country's territorial waters.

While entering harbour, manoeuvring and anchoring, mooring or berthing, you will be under the scrutiny of many eyes as you were when you left harbour. Some you will see but many will be watching you through binoculars and telescopes and remain un-noticed. Remember to behave in a seamanlike way, to be a credit to your boat and skipper.

When entering overcrowded harbours it may be more seaman-like to drop sail outside the harbour and motor in. Sometimes with a large yacht or a weak or unskilled crew it may be necessary to do the same in any harbour where normally a good skipper with an adequate crew will sail in and pick up mooring, berth or anchor without use of the engine. Some skippers keep the engine running in neutral in case it should be needed. It has always been considered an admission of lack of skill to use an engine to manoeuvre when it is possible to use sail.

It is beyond the scope of this book to go into the fine art of bringing a yacht up to a mooring or berth under various difficult conditions of wind and tide, but it is well worth watching how your yacht is manoeuvred and the behaviour of other yachts which may arrive later is also worth observing. It is sufficient for the new crew member to be on his toes and with his wits about him during these manoeuvres, so that he will learn by experience.

Furling sails

Sails can be furled simultaneously or individually, on entering harbour or after anchoring, mooring or berthing. The decision rests with the skipper and is involved with his plans of action. There must be no delay in getting sails down when ordered and the preparation and drill must be perfect. Imagine driving a car with it stuck in gear and no brakes in a crowded town. A yacht with a sail that won't come down is in the same predicament.

Mainsail

The preparation for furling the main consists of erecting the boom gallows or crutch, flaking down (laying out in loose coils) the main halyard falls and putting the sail ties on the boom. The weight of the boom is taken on the topping lift at the same time, so that when sail is lowered the boom will clear the gallows or crutch.

When all is ready the skipper will sail as close to the wind as he can bearing in mind local obstructions to navigation and other craft. On the instruction 'Lower main' or a suitable signal the crew member on the halyard lowers away handsomely (carefully), but must always watch the sail and falls to see that no snags or kinks develop. A crewman in the cockpit takes in the mainsheet and makes it up tight so that the boom does not swing around. This provides a firm handhold for the rest of the crew who are pulling the sail down, gathering it and pulling it aft. Normally only a rough bundle of sail along the boom will be made and sail ties quickly made up around it. The crew may then be required for other tasks and time will not permit a tidy harbour stow. Having secured the sail the topping lift will now be slackened away and the boom guided into its socket on the gallows or crutch taking in the slack in the mainsheet at the same time and cleating it up tight. If time permits the falls of the main halyard and the topping lift will be made up, the sheets will be coiled and hung from the gallows or boom end.

There are two neat harbour stow methods for furling the main, the flaked and the bagged. In the flaked method the sail is pulled aft and working from the clew towards the mast it is laid with the leech in a zig-zag pattern on top of the boom, the folds of the sail lying equally on each side. When the hoist is reached, the two sides of the sail are lifted and folded one on top of the other. In the bagging method all of the sail is put on one side of the boom and the crew stand on the other side and pull about a yard width of the foot of the sail over the boom to form a bag; the remaining body of the sail is pulled into this bag while being pulled aft at the same time. When it is all in this bag it is fisted (beaten with clenched fists) to get the air out so that it may be rolled up tightly on top of the boom. Sail battens if left in the sail must be laid individually along the length of the boom as the sail is rolled. If they are to be taken out, be careful as they can easily slip overboard. Sail ties should be tied round sail and boom at regular intervals with reef bows and the ends tucked neatly away.

Headsail

The headsail, having usually no boom, is much easier to lower and furl. The only preparations necessary are to flake down the falls of the halyard and to have some sail ties handy. This sail can be lowered without the skipper having to bring the yacht head-to-wind.

To lower the headsail one crew holds the halyard, another holds the foot of the sail. On the command 'Lower headsail' it is lowered quickly. The speed must be controlled so that the sail can be pulled on board and not allowed to dip in the water (36).

The sail can be left hanked on to the forestay and lashed into a bundle or along the rail out of the way, as explained above, or it can be unhanked from the stay, the tack, hoist and clew unshackled and the sail put into its bag with the head going in first and the tack last. A sail is only bagged if it is dry; if wet it should be passed below for drying later. Directly the halyard is unshackled it must be attached to some strong point such as the pulpit rail or an eyebolt. If it is left loose it will run up the mast out of reach, as will the falls if they are allowed to go free.

The sheets are usually unreeved and coiled up. The crewman in the cockpit should have undone the stopper knots in the sheet ends when he uncleated them while the sail was being lowered. The two sheets are usually coiled separately with the shackle lying between them. Leave the shackles on the sheets, halyard and tack, never on

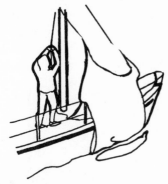

36   *When hauling on any rope never watch your hands but look at*
      what is being moved, in case things may be going wrong –
      ropes jammed, sails torn, or even danger to your crewmates

the sails as they will mark the cloth with rust spots. Finally coil away all falls and check that no marlin spikes, shackles, etc. are sculling around in the scuppers.

Anchoring

Anchoring is probably the easiest method of 'parking' a yacht, though the selection of the correct place to drop the anchor calls for skill and judgment on the part of the skipper. The preparation of the anchor has already been mentioned (35). As the position where the skipper has decided to drop anchor is approached the warning order 'Prepare to anchor' is given. If the anchor has been hung off,

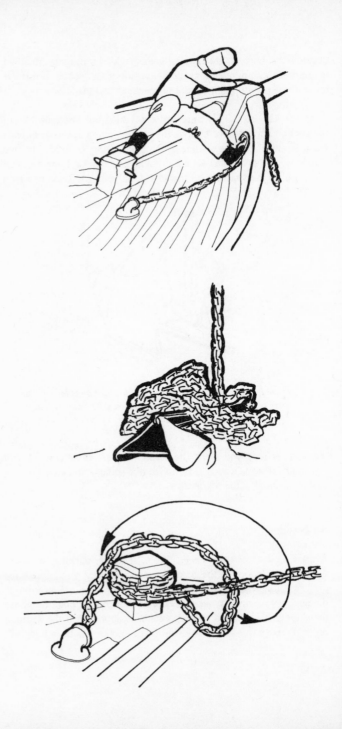

the foredeck crew stands by to release the winch clutch or cable brake. Otherwise, he lifts the anchor and carries it to the rail, making quite sure that he is not standing on or in a bight (loop) of the chain. On the order or sign 'Drop anchor' it is dropped well clear of the yacht's side while he and anyone on the foredeck make sure they avoid the chain, which will be running out fast and with much noise. The crewman then goes to the bow and slows the chain, after the anchor has hit bottom, by standing on it where it runs through the fairlead—not to be attempted with bare feet (37). It is quite easy thus to control the rate at which the chain runs out and to prevent it falling in a pile on top of the anchor as it lies on the bottom. A pile of chain on an anchor would stop it digging in correctly and cause it to drag (38). It is a great help to the foredeck hand if the skipper can tell him how deep the water is, as he can then stop the chain when the anchor is just resting on the bottom, reporting the fact and then paying out the rest of the chain slowly as the yacht drifts along. The skipper must also tell him how much scope (length) he wants laid out. This is usually at least three times the depth of the water at high water. Again a report should be made when it is fully out. The code of markings on the chain, which is usually every five fathoms (30 feet) must be known and understood by the crew dropping the anchor.

When the anchor chain is out the requisite amount the inboard end must be made up around the samson post or bitts (strong points on the deck). It is usually necessary to make several turns round this post and lock it in position by taking a loop from the part that runs to the anchor locker, passing it under the chain running to the anchor, and looping it back over the top of the post (39).

37 *To slow up the chain as it runs out when the anchor is dropped put a foot on it where it goes through the fairlead. This should only be attempted when wearing boots or shoes*

38 *Never let the chain run out uncontrolled. It may pile up on the anchor, foul it and prevent it digging in*

39 *When several turns have been made with the chain around the samson post take a bight (loop) of chain from the side not under strain and pass it under the chain going to the anchor. Now pass this bight over the top of the samson post and pull it tight. This will lock the chain in position so it cannot slip*

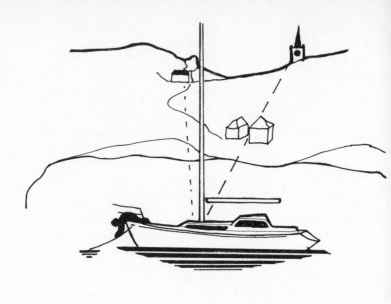

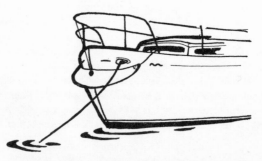

40 *When the anchor chain has been let out the required amount, hold the chain in the hand outside the bow fairlead. If the anchor is dragging it can be felt quite easily. Sometimes when below decks a dragging anchor will be heard as a rumbling sound. Bearings should be taken to prominent objects and recorded in the log. Sometimes a transit of two objects in line is more convenient. The yacht will move about to a certain extent with the wind and tide without dragging*

41 *A bow fender is rigged so that should the yacht ride up to its anchor or mooring chain under the influence of current and wind it will not scratch the hull*

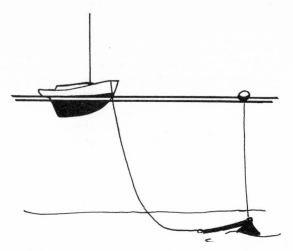

42 *If there is a possibility that the anchor may foul some obstruction on the seabed an anchor buoy line is rigged to the crown of the anchor so that it may be tripped clear of the obstruction by pulling on this line*

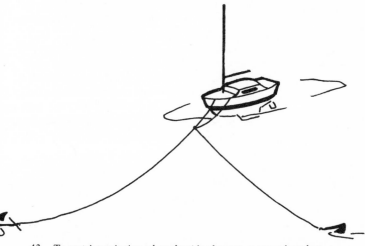

43 *To restrict swinging when the tide changes, a second anchor, usually the kedge, is laid up or down stream of the bower (main) anchor. The two chains or warps are then middled so that the yacht lies halfway between them. The two chains or warps are tied or shackled together and the join lowered over the side so that the yacht does not foul it as it swings*

It is now necessary to check whether the anchor is dragging (40). This can be felt by holding in the hand the chain outside the rail. If it is dragging vibration will be felt, and if you are below deck this may be heard as a rumbling sound. Do not make the mistake of thinking the anchor is dragging when it is only the chain being pulled over the ground by a change of wind or tide direction. Any dragging can also be checked visually by noting the bearings of fixed objects on the beam (at 90° to the fore-and-aft line) or by noting any objects on the beam that are in transit (in line). Do not worry about minor movements as the yacht will move up and back several yards as it pulls on its chain with varying strengths of tide and wind.

Under certain conditions of wind and tide the yacht will tend to rub her bows up against the chain, so that a bow fender must be rigged, or the chain near the bow parcelled with cloth to prevent the hull paint being scraped (41).

In harbours where there are known underwater obstructions which could trap an anchor, a tripping line is often rigged before dropping. This is a rope which is secured to the head of the anchor and it usually has an anchor buoy on the other end (42). If the anchor becomes caught a pull on this line should free it.

Sometimes in restricted waters it will be necessary to drop a second or kedge anchor on a rope warp to prevent the yacht swinging all over the place. In this case the main anchor chain will be let out for an extra ten fathoms or more, and when the yacht has set back on this the kedge is dropped over the stern. The main chain is then brought back and the kedge warp paid (let) out until the yacht lies nearly middled (halfway) between the two anchors. The kedge warp is then brought forward and tied to the main anchor chain with a cable knot, and the anchor chain let out a little more so that this knot lies under the surface of the water and the two anchor lines do not twist round each other (43).

When the yacht is lying to a single anchor and a gale blows up or it is very rough, the use of an anchor chain weight or chum helps to prevent her snubbing (jerking) at the anchor. A heavy weight is shackled to a saddle and this is slid down the chain for a few fathoms on a line. As the yacht pulls back it has to lift this weight to straighten the curve in the chain, thereby snubbing less violently. The weight also keeps the anchor stock at a low and more effective angle (44).

So far we have referred to anchor chain, but many yachts today use nylon or similar lines instead of chain, frequently with a few fathoms of chain next to the anchor to prevent the fibre chafing on the bottom. The principles of use are the same as explained for chain, but warps tend to snarl up and chafe much more easily than chain so extra care is needed.

If by any chance you anchor or moor in a fairway where other boats will pass, a black ball-shaped object should be hoisted in or near the fore-rigging by day and a white riding light kept burning there by night to indicate that you are at anchor (45). This a legal obligation which is sometimes forgotten.

Berthing

The necessary preparations for berthing have already been mentioned; fenders, lines and the heaving line, boat hook and spare line are to hand. The skipper will not be certain how he will be coming alongside the quay, pontoon or pier until he has seen it and any obstructions there may be, such as other craft already berthed.

When he has made his plan he will tell the crew which side he will want the fenders. The crew, without obstructing the skipper's line of sight, must tie these fenders to strong points along the side indicated. It is usual to tie these fenders with two round turns and a half hitch to the stanchions so that they hang between the rail and water evenly spaced along the midship section. The height and position of the fenders may have to be adjusted when close alongside and the actual projections which could damage the hull can be seen. The bow and stern crewmen should now lead the fixed ends of the bow and stern lines over the rails and back through their respective fairleads (46). It is advisable to have about two fathoms (12 feet) off the top of the coil in hand and ready to pass up to anyone on the quayside—more may be necessary. Check as always that these lines are free, ready to run and will not snarl up at the crucial moment.

As the yacht approaches the quay one crew member with a spare fender stands by ready to place it between the yacht and any obstruction should it be needed. In the same manner another stands ready with the boat hook.

The skipper has the choice of a number of ways for coming

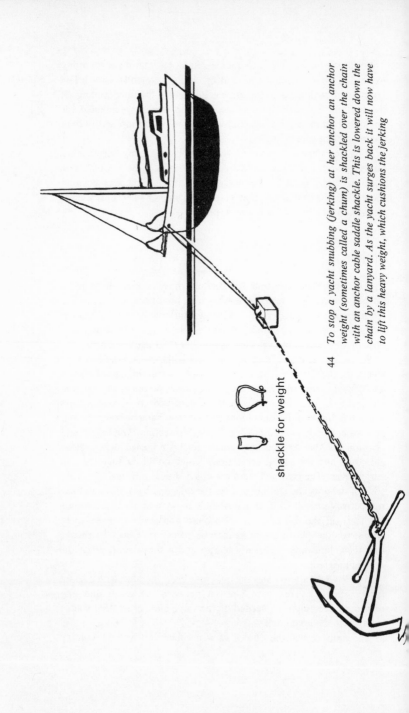

shackle for weight

44 To stop a yacht snubbing (jerking) at her anchor an anchor weight (sometimes called a chum) is shackled over the chain with an anchor cable saddle shackle. This is lowered down the chain by a lanyard. As the yacht surges back it will now have to lift this heavy weight, which cushions the jerking

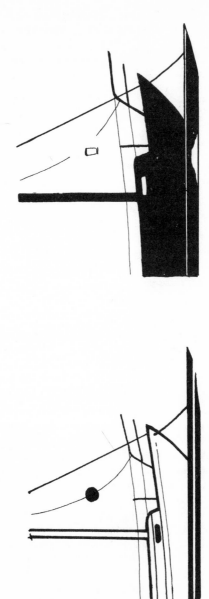

45 When anchored in or near a fairway a black ball-shaped object should be hoisted near the bow by day, and a white light which can shine all round by night

alongside, each with minor variations depending on the situation. There is no fixed drill but the following is a basic outline.

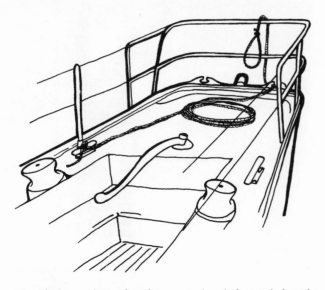

46 *The bow and stern lines have one end made fast on deck, and are coiled down to run out without a snarl-up, with large bowlines tied in the free ends*

The afterdeck crew member, with the stern line in hand, stands near the shrouds (rigging supporting the mast at the side) and jumps onto the quay as soon as possible and places the loop quickly over a suitable bollard (iron or wood post). He then runs forward along the quay and collects the bow line from the foredeck crewman and makes it fast in the same way. Meanwhile the rest of the crew will be fending the yacht off from the quay or any other obstructions and also taking in the bow and stern lines or allowing them to surge (slip) around a strong cleat or samson post to slow the yacht, then making them fast on board. The bow and stern lines are adjusted so that they are as long as possible and approximately the same length, and the yacht is lying where the skipper wants her. Remember, if the bow is pulled too far in towards the quay the yacht will pivot around its fenders, the stern will be pushed out, and vice versa. This is a good example of the necessity to keep an eye on what the other crew are doing and not to pull against them.

The two springs, which run in the opposite direction to the bow and stern lines, are now put out and, if necessary, two breast lines can be lead direct from the mast and the cockpit to the quay (5). It will be realised that if this is a tidal harbour some of these lines and springs may have to be adjusted as the yacht rises and falls. This

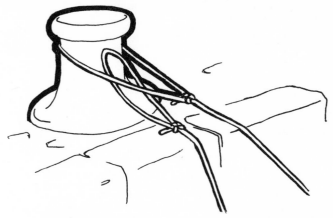

47 *Should you have to secure a line to a bollard that already has another line over it, make a large bowline loop, pass this under and up through the other loops, and over the top of the bollard. Either line can then be removed without disturbing the other*

applies especially to short ropes such as breast lines, and it may be necessary to have a crewman permanently on watch to adjust them.

Sometimes it may be necessary to lie outside another yacht. In this case, when the skipper has brought your yacht alongside, make fast to the other craft with two breast lines and two springs. Then take your bow and stern lines to the bollards on the quay in the normal manner. You may find another yacht already has lines on the bollard that you wish to use, in which case pass the loop of your line under and up through the loop(s) of the other lines and then over the bollard (47). In this way yachts can remove their warps without disturbing others. If some other yacht wants to lie outside you, help them to make fast as shown above making sure that they have put out their own bow and stern lines to the quay. It is most unwise to have a double load on one set of lines should the weather blow up.

If you wish to leave before the boat on the outside it will be necessary to slip either her bow or stern line in order to get out. Pass this line around your yacht and back to the quay. Leave a crew member on board to readjust their lines; you can pick him up later. Remember that you are responsible for the other yacht in the absence of her crew.

Drying out in a berth

While dealing with berthing it is appropriate to consider the actions needed when drying out against the quay wall (48). The most

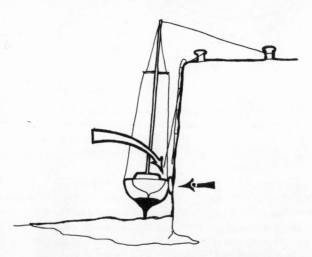

48　*When a yacht has to dry out alongside a quay it is necessary to place portable weights such as the anchor and chain along the deck near to the quay. Fenders and perhaps a griping spar (a length of wood) are placed between the yacht and the wall. The main halyard is attached to a strong point ashore (do not forget to adjust this as the tide rises and falls). A rope ladder to get ashore may also be rigged*

important thing is to ensure that as the water recedes the yacht will lean against the quay and will not lean or fall outwards onto her side. Usually the anchor and all the chain from the anchor locker is flaked down on the sidedeck nearest the quay, which will give you enough heel (lean) to ensure that she dries out correctly. As a precaution the main halyard can be unshackled and attached to a strong point ashore. Remember that this will need slacking off as the yacht rises with the tide.

Crew often forget that when dried out the heads (W.C.) cannot be operated, also that it may be a difficult climb from deck to quay and back. A rope ladder rigged to the quay while still afloat is worth having.

Do not sit with all your friends on the side of the deck away from the quay, as this may cause the yacht to fall over on her side.

Berthing stern-to

In some harbours it may be necessary to berth stern-to the quay with the bow pointing out at right angles. It is usual to drop an anchor or to pick up a mooring buoy away from the quay and for the skipper to manoeuvre the yacht stern first into a gap between the other yachts already in position. This is a difficult operation and considerable assistance can be given by the crew in using fenders in an intelligent way and helping manually to ease the yacht into the berth (49). When in position two stern lines are taken to the quay and fenders are put out on both sides. Breast lines and springs to the yachts on either side will control any swing and undue bumping.

Mooring to a buoy

The preparation for mooring is quite simple. All that is required is a short length of line and a boat hook. Provided the skipper is skilful enough to bring his yacht to a halt with the buoy within reach of his crew, mooring is very easy to accomplish. The end of the line should be made fast to a strong cleat on the foredeck and passed under the rail and through a bow fairlead. The free end should be long enough to pass through the eye on the mooring buoy and back

93

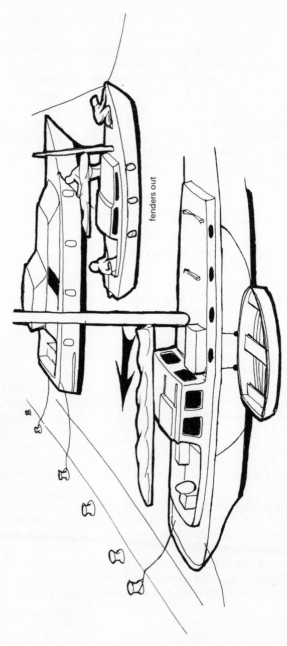

fenders out

49 Berthing stern-to requires careful manoeuvring by the skipper and intelligent teamwork by the crew. The yacht's bow is first anchored, or moored to a buoy, and she is then eased astern into her berth by using the engine, or manually by the crew, the rate being controlled by the crewman on the foredeck paying out the anchor chain or mooring line

under the rail through the fairlead to a cleat (3) with about a fathom (six feet) to spare.

As the mooring is approached the crew member with the line lies down on the deck right up in the bow (not on the line) so that he can easily reach the buoy. A second man with the boat hook in hand signals to the skipper the direction and distance to the buoy. It will be appreciated that in a yacht of any size, the bow will hide the buoy from the skipper as the yacht nears it. An agreed code of signals is necessary. Probably the easiest method is for the crewman with the boat hook to use it to point at the buoy (50). The larger yachts will need more comprehensive signals.

Directly the end of the line has been passed through the eye on the buoy it is quickly pulled back on board through the fairlead and made fast to the samson post or cleat. It is important that this

50 *As the yacht approaches its mooring a crewman with one end of the mooring line in hand (the other end being secured to a cleat) lies down in the bow ready to pass it through the eye on top of the mooring buoy. A second crewman stands over him with the boathook pointing at the buoy to give guidance to the skipper*

operation is done as fast as possible as the yacht usually has a little way on her and unless the line is made fast quickly it may be pulled back out of the grasp of the crew. The novice will be surprised at the strength needed to stop a slow-moving yacht and he must never expect to stop it unless he has taken a turn in the line around a strong point. With two men working on the foredeck this operation can be carried out swiftly.

Sometimes the yacht is going too fast or the buoy is beyond the reach of the crewman with the line. In this case the boat hook is used to pull the buoy within his grasp. If he still fails to reach it and the yacht continues past the buoy, the boat hook must be kept in the buoy and the crewman concerned walks aft with it to the cockpit. From there another attempt can be made to pass a spare warp through its eye. If successful it will be necessary to be very quick getting the two ends of this warp secured to cleats, taking care to see that they have a fair lead under the rails that will not damage the stanchions.

There is, however, nothing wrong with picking up a mooring alongside or from the cockpit. It is the normal drill when single-handed or with a very light crew. It is also easier for the skipper to see the buoy during the manoeuvre. Care is necessary in using this procedure in strong winds, currents or streams as the yacht may get out of control.

Having secured the buoy on a short scope (length of rope) under the bows, it is necessary to replace the line with either the anchor chain or a short length of chain specially kept for the purpose. The cable should be shackled to the buoy and secured around the samson post or bitts, and the rope can then be cast off. Unless it is a special mooring buoy with a steel rod right through it, it will be necessary to shackle the chain to the mooring chain under the buoy, and the use of the dinghy will make this operation easier. Some buoys have a short length of rope or light cable attached to the heavy mooring chain to enable it to be lifted so that the yacht's chain can be attached to its end. The bow fender should now be rigged.

If the buoy has a small pick-up buoy attached this should be taken on board through the fairlead and tied to the forestay. This pick-up buoy is handy because when approaching the mooring buoy it can be picked up easily and made fast in the same manner as a line.

Sometimes in restricted waters it will be necessary to moor between two buoys. Usually these are connected with a light line and once the yacht is secured to one the other can be brought alongside by pulling on this rope.

It is possible to moor to a buoy and have an anchor out to prevent swinging to the tidal stream. If the skipper moors first with a long line and then, letting this out, manoeuvres to where he wants to drop his anchor, all that is then necessary is to haul back on the line while paying out the anchor chain to adjust his position. This manoeuvre can be undertaken in the opposite way, i.e. anchoring, then paying out the chain while moving towards the buoy and finally making fast to it. The mooring chain should be as short as possible and the buoy close to the bow, or hoisted out of the water. Never moor with a long line or chain because at certain states of the wind and tide the yacht will ride up to the buoy and scratch the paint. It also increases the area covered by the yacht and it may bump a nearby boat.

Mooring to piles

In many crowded harbours yachts are moored bow to stern to piles (large mooring posts) with usually up to four yachts per pair of posts. When other yachts are already in position on the piles the skipper has only to come alongside the outside yacht and then to make fast to her with breast lines and springs. By using the dinghy the bow and stern lines are taken to the piles and made fast. A good-sized loop tied with a bowline is advised as the lines may get trapped and be lying under water at high tide. Should the skipper want to leave then, if the knot cannot be hauled to the surface someone will have to swim down for it.

If the piles are unoccupied when you arrive the skipper will lay the yacht's bow alongside one of the posts so that the bow line may be passed around it. This line must either be tied with a large loop or both ends brought back aboard and made fast.

It may be possible to manoeuvre the stern back to the other post simply by letting out the bow line, or a dinghy may be used to take the line. It is advisable to have fenders out on both sides when moored to piles as other craft may come alongside you at any time.

Warping ship

Before the days of engines ships had to be moved inside harbours by the use of warps (long lengths of heavy rope), often with very limited manpower. Warping is becoming a lost art as auxiliary engines become more and more reliable. This is regrettable because yacht engines do fail, and there are occasions such as when leaving a crowded berth late at night when warping is essential in order not to disturb others.

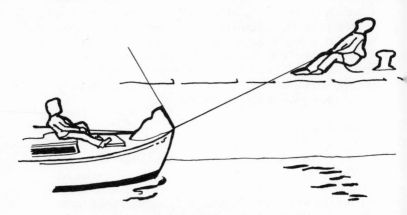

51 *Be quite clear who is going to do the pulling and who is going to make the line fast. Do not indulge in a tug of war!*

When warping keep the following in mind: a yacht is a heavy object and it takes a long steady pull to get it moving; conversely, once moving it will take a similar effort to stop it. Be quite clear who is going to do the pulling and do not be caught in the ridiculous predicament of carrying out a tug-of-war with some of the crew on the yacht and the rest on land (51). One end or the other according to circumstances should be made fast. The end that is free should be kept untangled and whenever possible should have a half turn round some strong point so that should the pull become too great the strain can be taken on this. This is vitally important when paying out a warp as even a small yacht in a strong wind or tidal stream can produce a pull too great for a man to hold.

Warping is always done slowly, with care and deliberation and step by step; any attempt to hurry can easily result in trouble and damage.

Sometimes it may be essential to send off a warp to some distant point by boat. When this is done the warp should be coiled down in the dinghy so that as it is rowed away from the yacht the warp pays out. If this warp is to be placed round a bollard or something similar then a large bowline should be placed in the end before it is lowered into the dinghy, with the bowline at the bottom.

One of the arts of warping is to make use of the stream running at the time, and the wind; used intelligently these will often move the yacht, leaving the crew free to control the movement.

If it is necessary to pull heavily on a warp this should be done by leaning back on the rope with a straight back (51). The basic pull should come from the legs and not from the arms or back.

A lot of effort is saved if warps are doubled so that they can be slipped when required by letting go one end and pulling all back on board by the other.

H

8 Harbour Work

Many yachts can be seen these days in the harbours around our coast left in a dirty, untidy and sometimes dangerous state. The only deduction that can be made is that the skippers and crew are either completely inexperienced or simply idle. The skipper and crew of a yacht are judged by the way their boat is kept and some would be amazed at the comments passed by others about them and the condition of their yacht.

Harbour stow

It is the good crewman's job to see that the yacht is clean and properly stowed directly she is anchored, berthed or moored. The correct method for stowing sails has already been described and stowing may have been done before the harbour is reached. Have another critical look: it may be necessary to unfurl and restow. The sail should be a smooth tapering roll with neat sail ties spaced at equal intervals along the boom. Look at the mainsheet: is it secure in a neat coil on the end of the boom? All unwanted ropes and warps should be coiled and taken below. The free ends of the lines in use and the falls of halyards should be neatly coiled. Fenders if in use should be equally spaced and if possible hung at the same height. Above all, the deck, cockpit and hull should be cleaned down and any brightwork polished.

It is usual to tie the halyards back to the shrouds so that they do not frap (bang) against the mast making a disturbing noise which is not only an annoyance to the crew but also to neighbouring yachts.

Finally have a good look around and see if your yacht is the smartest in the harbour. If it is not do something about it.

Flags

The Q flag and the courtesy ensign have already been mentioned. Once the Customs and Immigration officers have visited the yacht the Q flag can be hauled down and stowed. The courtesy ensign will remain flying from the starboard signal halyard by day while the yacht is in territorial waters. At the stern the yacht's national ensign will be flying. This is kept flying between 8 o'clock in the morning and sunset, while in harbour. It should always be struck (hauled down) at sunset or when the crew leaves the yacht and does not expect to be back until after sunset. In some northern estuaries where the sunset is very late colours are struck at 9 o'clock in the evening. The burgee flying from the top of the mast is treated in the same way as the ensign unless the skipper is a flag officer, in which case his special flag is kept flying at all times while he is with the yacht.

The courtesy ensign is also struck and hoisted at the same time as the yacht's ensign and burgee. It is normal to take the actual time of striking colours from the senior service, club or yacht in the harbour. Punctillious observation of flag etiquette is yet another sign of a good crewman. At sea flags need only be worn when in sight of the coast or other ships but because our coastal waters are so crowded with shipping it is usual to keep the yacht's ensign flying while at sea. The burgee or flag officer's flag is also kept flying to indicate the direction of the wind.

While at sea should you pass one of HM ships or a flag officer's yacht the ensign should be dipped (hauled two-thirds down), and when acknowledged by a similar action of the other ship it should be hoisted again. Smart drill on the counter of a small yacht is difficult but do your best under the circumstances.

Dinghy work

A good crewman must be expert with the pulling dinghy and should get all the practice he can by using the dinghy whenever possible. If the opportunity arises to practice with a dinghy before he goes on his first cruise he is well advised to make the best possible use of it. Even a few hours sculling around on a seaside boating pool will be of great value.

The average yacht's dinghy is small (about 6-9 feet) and of wood or fibreglass construction, or an inflatable.

Boarding

Rigid dinghies are unstable and when getting in or out the weight of one's body must be in the centre of the boat. While in the dinghy always sit down and keep weight as low as possible; never move about violently or quickly or lean out over the side (52).

Never jump into a dinghy, as you may go through the bottom or cause other structural damage. The best way to get into a dinghy from a high-sided yacht or pontoon is backwards. Face the yacht and take hold of some strong point, then with one foot on the yacht's rail and the other extended out behind you towards the centre of the dinghy, lower yourself in. Be very careful handing parcels in and out of the dinghy if they are bulky and heavy, especially if there is a sea running. It is advisable to tie a rope around the parcel and to have the free end secured to a strong point before trans-shipping awkward loads.

Overloading

If a dinghy is overloaded it becomes even more unstable and dangerous, especially if the freeboard is reduced to a few inches, and any little waves can lap over the gunwale (edge) and fill the dinghy. This is particularly important to remember after dark. There have been a considerable number of accidents caused by crews returning after an evening's celebrations ashore in overloaded dinghies.

Pneumatic dinghies

An inflatable dinghy in this respect is much safer than a rigid dinghy as it is possible to stand on the edge without capsizing it,

52 *If you stand on the edge of a dinghy it will capsize and you will end up in the water. Never stand up in a dinghy; keep your weight as low as possible*

and it will remain afloat even when filled with water. However, rubber dinghies do not row as easily and the crew often get splashed because they are so low in the water. It is virtually impossible to make any headway rowing a rubber dinghy against waves and a strong wind.

Rowing

To explain how to row in a book is equivalent to explaining how to walk as it is so natural. You just sit with your back to the bow, which is also the direction of travel, dip the oar blades into the water and pull until the oars make an angle of about 45° with the centreline of the boat. Then by pushing down on the handles and away from you bring the blades out of the water and back towards the bow until they again make an angle of about 45°, then by raising the hands dip the blades in the water again ready for the next stroke. A little practice makes it virtually an automatic action.

It is usual to row from the midship thwart (seat) with passengers suitably distributed in the bow and stern so that the trim (balance) is correct. However, if there is only one passenger on board, the rowing position may be changed to the forward thwart to correct the trim.

Rowing a small dinghy in a short choppy sea requires a different technique to that employed on calm waters. The stroke is short and quick, the blade is not fully feathered, the arms not the back do most of the work, and the blades are lifted much higher out of the water.

Sculling with a single oar in the transom is a useful technique to learn. The dinghy can be propelled very efficiently in this way. Another method worth trying is to row facing the bow while kneeling on the centre thwart, or in a larger dinghy from a standing position. There are times when these variations are invaluable.

Coming alongside

It is at once apparent to the onlooker how good an oarsman you are when you bring a dinghy alongside a yacht or quay. The expert arrives without fuss and bother and the dinghy comes to a stop a few inches from the yacht exactly where it should. The secret, as with many skills, is practice and a little basic knowledge.

As the approach is made, assess the effects of the tidal stream and the wind on the dinghy. This can often be done while passing other yachts and buoys on the way. If time permits have a practice run by coming alongside a buoy. Approach the yacht at an angle of about 45° and against the current or wind, whichever has the stronger effect on the dinghy. Aim to come alongside where the yacht's rail is lowest, usually just forward of the cockpit. Generate enough momentum to bring the dinghy alongside and unship (take into the dinghy) the oar nearest the yacht at the same time removing the rowlock (a rowlock in its socket can score the yacht's paintwork). As the dinghy reaches the yacht give a pull on the remaining oar to bring her alongside then catch hold of the yacht's rail and unship the remaining oar and rowlock. Make the painter fast to the yacht and secure the oars by passing the rowlocks on their lanyards round them several times.

A similar procedure is adopted coming alongside the quay. If, however, there is a sea running and you are coming alongside steps be careful not to be swept onto them by a wave as the dinghy may well capsize as the wave recedes.

Slipping

Before even getting into the dinghy to go ashore, assess the effect of wind and tide and make a plan. Untie the painter and pass it around a suitable stanchion (rail) and hold the end. Keeping a hold on the painter get into the dinghy and ship the rowlock and oar on the side away from the yacht. Pull the painter into the dinghy and push off from the yacht, shipping the other oar as soon as possible.

Rowing across a current

If the yacht is moored in midstream set off for the shore at 45° upstream of the course that you want and move crab-wise across the current. If you are being swept off the correct course do not be dismayed but continue until very close inshore where the current is less, then row parallel to the bank. Similarly, when you want to return to the yacht row against the current while close inshore until well upstream of the yacht. Then set off into midstream aiming for a point well above the yacht so that you will drift down to her. If you have not made enough allowance for the current you may well miss the yacht and be forced to repeat the whole procedure again. This is particularly important to remember with a rubber dinghy which cannot be rowed very fast but is easily blown by the wind. Use a transit of two points near the direction in which you wish to travel to assess progress.

Securing alongside

A dinghy must be secured alongside a yacht so that it cannot damage it by rubbing against it or by getting caught under the counter (overhanging stern). The only really satisfactory way is to secure it alongside lying against small fenders with bow and stern painters made up to the yacht (49). An alternative is to stand it off by tying the stern painter to something else, say another yacht, dolphin or quay. A bucket tied to a short line and put out over the stern of a dinghy will hold it away from the yacht while the current is strong but the wind will take charge once the current goes slack.

Securing ashore

The rise and fall of the tide is an additional factor to watch out for when securing your boat ashore. The wind and current should also be considered, as should the position of other yachts' tenders already ashore.

In some areas, notably around the Channel Islands, the rise and fall of the tide can be over thirty feet. It is embarrassing to return to the quay to find your dinghy suspended in the air by its painter, or the knot in the end several feet under water.

When possible it is best to pull or lift the dinghy ashore making sure that it is parked above the high water mark and that it and its oars are secured. When securing your dinghy have consideration for others who may come in after you and leave enough room for them at the landing place.

An outboard for a dinghy is a mixed blessing. It enables greater distances between yacht and shore to be covered quickly and without effort but it is a bulky oily nuisance when stowed on board the yacht. It is liable to loss overboard during trans-shipment between yacht and dinghy and ashore motors are a temptation to thieves. Finally when needed urgently they usually fail to start. Always have a lanyard attached to the ouboard and make certain it is firmly secured to the yacht when transferring it from yacht to dinghy and vice versa. Once dropped overboard you will find it very difficult to recover. Most harbours are well lined with lost outboards.

Yacht engines

The engines on yachts are of many makes and designs and the ways in which they are fitted vary. It is, therefore, impossible to make any detailed observations. In general yacht engines are working in an unsatisfactory environment, in wet salt air in a confined space where it is difficult to clean and maintain them. Deterioration can take place rapidly, especially as they are often left for long periods without being started. If the good crewman is given the task of looking after the engine he must find out about all or some of the following.

Fuel: tank, tap, filter(s); are they clean? Fuel lines, carburetter/injector pump.

Ignition: magneto/coil leads; are they clean and dry? Spark plugs, gaps, clean and dry? Is there a shorting switch and/or isolator switch? Note that electricity will pass through salt water and cause shorts.

Cooling: water inlet cock and filter clear? Water pump greased? Water outlet correct (usually leads into the exhaust to keep it cool) and functioning?

Oil: filler, dipstick, oil level. When was oil last changed and filter cleaned?

Greasing: greasing and oiling points, where are they and when to be greased? Water pump grease cap and stern gland greaser.

Charging: dynamo, voltage control and charging system. Accumulators, topped up and cleaned?

Controls: throttle, choke, on/off switch, neutral and astern gear.

Instruments: ammeter, oil pressure gauge, hour metre, temperature gauge.

Drills: for starting and stopping the engine; gear controls for going ahead, neutral and astern and how they work. If possible a detailed study of the engine handbook is invaluable, otherwise get verbal instruction from the skipper.

53 *Some skippers treat the auxiliary engine as a 'devil in the bilge', never to be disturbed or attended to. They then complain when it fails at some crucial moment. Look after the black devil and it will look after you!*

There are a number of skippers who are very anti-engines and virtually refuse to have anything to do with them, but expect them to perform reliably when required. This can be dangerous as engines treated in this way nearly always fail at some crucial moment when they are really needed. Crewmen with knowledge and experience of car engines soon understand marine versions and will be amazed at some of the Heath Robinson installations that they will find.

It is unlikely that the crew will be allowed to manoeuvre the yacht under power, but should the eventuality occur the following notes will help.

Always remember that the yacht takes time to gain and lose speed due to its weight and momentum. A normal propeller is not nearly so efficient going astern as it is going ahead so do not expect the boat to slow up quickly when astern gear is engaged.

When going slowly a propeller will slip and fail to grip the water if too much throttle is applied. Use the right amount of throttle so that the propeller turns fast but does not race.

All single propellers tend to pull the stern to one side, because when the blades are at the bottom they are in water which offers

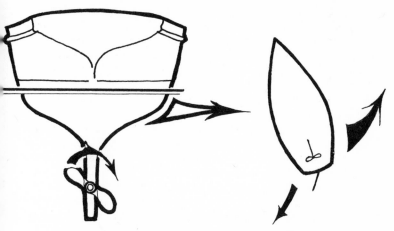

54 *At slow speeds a clockwise rotating (right-handed) propeller will pull the stern to starboard, as it has more effect in the water at the bottom of its rotation. At the top the hull also interferes with its efficiency*

55 *When it is necessary to turn a yacht in a small space a short sharp burst of the engine in ahead with the rudder hard over will kick the stern around. A touch of astern with the rudder held amidships will stop any headway*

greater resistance, increasing their effect. When at the top, the blades are less efficient as they are closer to the hull. A propeller rotating clockwise when viewed from aft will pull the stern to starboard (54).

When it is necessary to make a tight turn, put the helm over and give a short burst in ahead to swing the yacht round. A touch of slow astern with no helm will prevent her going too far forward (55).

Remember that when going astern the effect of the rudder is reversed. If you can visualise the position of the blade of the rudder under the water this will help you to realise what is occurring. Watch out for any ropes, painters, log lines, etc that might foul the propeller.

Going ashore

Once the Customs and Immigration officers have cleared the yacht and the many and varied chores on board have been completed the crew will be keen to go ashore. If anchored or moored, some plan of action is needed so that all the crew can not only get to the shore but back on board again. It is easy to leave someone marooned on shore or on board if there is only one dinghy and it is not large enough to take the whole crew at once.

When ashore do not forget to keep a check on the route back to your dinghy and also on the time. In the first flush of looking round an exciting foreign town it is easy to forget both and to arrive back late to find an irate skipper waiting for you.

Your dress and behaviour should be suitable for the occasion and time of day. Moderation in dress and behaviour is essential. Remember that as a foreigner you will be under constant surveillance by the locals (56).

When going ashore do not form a permanent clique with a particular friend or group of friends to the exclusion of other crew members. This division may develop into impossible situations on board and ruin the cruise for all. A little commonsense in this matter will prevent such divisions developing. On the other hand there are crew who sometimes like to go off on their own and do not wish to go round the town in a group. Let them go; privacy is a rare thing on a yacht and it is nice to be alone for a change.

It is probable that stores will have to be bought for the yacht and it is usual for either a kitty to be arranged to which everyone subscribes a fixed amount, or some accounting system organised. Make quite certain that you know all about it and how it is run; ask the skipper right out—he will not mind and it is miserable not knowing how much money you may have to spend and when.

Take care how much you eat and drink ashore. It is very easy to over-indulge and ruin your holiday with an upset stomach.

56 *Moderation in dress and behaviour is essential ashore. Remember that you are a foreigner when abroad*

If you purchase any dutiable items such as spirits, perfume, cigarettes and tobacco bear in mind the maximum amounts that you are allowed to bring home free of duty and do not embarrass your skipper by having any in excess when you return to the UK, and do not fail to declare what you have bought.

Even if you only have a few words of the language of the country that you visit, make use of them and you will be surprised at the help and co-operation that you will get. Foreigners loathe those British who shout their views and requirements at the top of their voices in English, and react in the same way as we would.

9 Domestic

Cooking

It is usual for all members of a crew to take their turn in the galley and to prepare and cook meals, unless in the lucky position of having a real sea cook aboard, who will cook all meals. In this case it is customary for the crew to help with the preparation of the food by undertaking such jobs as potato peeling. It is an almost unwritten law that the cook is excused washing up, but he is usually expected to clean up any mess on the stove or in the galley left as a result of his labours. A new crew member is well advised to acquire a little knowledge of cooking methods before his first trip but should concentrate on simple basic dishes. In normal conditions ordinary non-greasy, non-rich food is undoubtedly the best for meals at sea especially when some of the crew may be feeling queasy. If possible meals at sea should be cooked by someone who is feeling fit, as cooking a meal usually induces seasickness. In the event of seasickness sufferers can sometimes be persuaded to drink Bovril and to munch cream crackers or similar foods which may effect a cure.

Cooking in a galley in a small boat is in itself somewhat difficult, but to do the same in a seaway is an art and a struggle. All that can be advised is to stick to very simple things to cook like thick soup, hash, etc which require the minimum of preparation, cooking and serving, but at the same time are hot and filling. Take great care that the hot food does not scald the cook if the pan slips off the stove. If in a bathing dress an apron should be worn. Cups, pans and dishes should never be more than half full, otherwise they will slop over. Fiddles (rails) should be put round the stove and table, to prevent plates etc sliding off. A wet cloth laid over a table has the same effect.

It is often a good idea to have the last meal of the day at sunset or at change of watch and to have the cook prepare hot soup in Thermos containers for consumption during the watches of the night. This prevents the sleepers being disturbed by cooking operations and galley lights in the night.

As already mentioned, it is important to replace everything in its correct place in the galley so that the next cook can find things with no waste of time. It is also most essential to keep everything scrupulously clean and never to leave dirty dishes around at any time, especially at sea when extra effort is needed to carry out this task. The restricted amount of water and stowage space makes it difficult to achieve these aims. Sometimes salt water has to be used for washing up crockery and pans but most liquid household detergents will work in salt water.

The stowage and disposal of garbage presents a problem on a yacht in harbour where it must not be thrown over the side. Most harbours today have garbage bins ashore and a bucket or some such container must be taken ashore when full. When several miles from land garbage is usually disposed of over the side, but make certain that all tins are pierced at both ends and bottles are filled with water so that they sink at once. Plastic bags and sheets must be weighted so that they sink as they are dangerous floating on the surface or just below the surface where they can foul propellers and water intakes.

Finally there are many good books on the subject of cooking in yachts which are worth reading and having handy on board.

Bunking

The new crewman will find himself allocated to a bunk on arrival (58). This could be a pipe cot in the forecastle consisting of a sheet of canvas stretched over a metal frame, which is quite comfortable to sleep on in harbour but subject to violent motion at sea as the bow of the ship rides over the waves. It is usual then for the occupants of the forecastle to share the bunks further aft, in turns with the rightful owners. The practice is often referred to as 'warm bunking'. The bunks amidships will usually be the seats in the saloon, which may have another bunk outboard of them, referred to as a pilot berth. These are the most comfortable bunks and are out of the way of the traffic that moves through the saloon. Further aft other bunks may be found which extend in part under the cockpit seats, termed quarter berths, and these are comfortable. In some yachts there may be a separate aft cabin with a pair of bunks and perhaps separate cabins amidships.

A sleeping bag with a washable liner is the best form of bedding for use on a yacht, as ordinary sheets and blankets are difficult to use, and the fluff that comes off blankets finds its way into the bilges and can block the pumps.

Pillows are a problem to carry around so most owners have some on board for visiting crews. All bedding is very susceptible to wet and damp so a large strong plastic bag to keep it in when not in use is desirable. Make use of any opportunity of a dry sunny day to air bedding, having first ascertained that the skipper has no objections, and remember to secure it well as it can easily blow over the side.

Yacht's bunks are equipped with boards or canvas which can be erected on the inboard side of the bunk when at sea so that the occupant does not roll out when the yacht heels over. These bunkboards have additional advantages in that they also prevent bedding and clothing slipping off onto the floor.

When in harbour or day sailing bedding should be stowed away. Most skippers will insist on this, especially the bedding from the bunks in the saloon.

Heads

In past ages the crews of sailing ships used to relieve themselves over the side of the bow of the ship, hence the term 'heads' for the W.C. on a yacht. The normal heads installed on yachts are complex pieces of apparatus consisting of pumps and valves for clean water and another set for the disposal of waste under water. It is normal for the skipper or mate to explain the intricacies of the system to all new crew on arrival. In most designs it is mandatory to turn off the clean water inlet stop valve because if left open it may allow water to flow into the bilges and could sink the yacht. It may also be essential to shut off the outlet stop valve in some yachts. All yacht's heads are subject to blockage if unnatural things are put down them; matchsticks, toothpaste caps or razor blades can jam valves. Taking the system to bits to clear the blockage is a revolting job which is usually allocated to the person who caused the trouble. So use the heads intelligently, with consideration for others in keeping them clean. In very small yachts do not be surprised to find that the heads consist of a bucket in the fore part of the cabin as there is no room for a separate compartment.

In many yachts at sea or at night in harbour it is usual for the crew, often both male and female, to use the original heads as opposed to the modern contrivance below decks. The pulpit might have been designed for this very purpose. Care must be exercised at sea and sometimes the lee shrouds or the stern pulpit and aft stay may be less dangerous places to use.

Washing and shaving

Personal washing and shaving present a problem on a small yacht as there is not enough room for all to perform their ablutions at the same time, and indeed in most yachts there is very little room for even one person. A goodly supply of small plastic basins will enable some of the crew to wash in the cockpit or on deck while others spread around the yacht can do the same below. The limited supply of fresh water is another factor to be considered and a bath on deck using buckets of salt water is not to be despised as an alternative. Luckily most yacht clubs have showers and washing facilities and the hotels at harbours are used to yachtsmen coming ashore asking for baths.

The washing of clothing is limited by the supply of water on board and the possibilities of drying afterwards. Some skippers will not let their yacht be decorated from bow to stern with assorted smalls while in harbour, while others have no objection. It is advisable to find out his views before getting busy with the washtub. The use of launderettes, which are to be found at most ports, can be one solution.

The drying of towels and dishcloths from the galley is a problem if they cannot be hung out to dry, as a salty atmosphere tends to keep damp things damp. Disposable towels are worth considering.

Housework

The standard of cleanliness varies from yacht to yacht and advice can only be given as to what should be done as a matter of routine. Your skipper will normally give the necessary orders.

Yachts, like houses, soon get dirty when occupied and once a day they have to be swept out and dusted below decks. If there is any brasswork this will have to be polished and in some yachts it will also be necessary to scrub the floors. The galley area will have to be cleaned out thoroughly and the heads compartment washed down once a day. There is a simple and foolproof way of telling if a yacht is clean: sniff the air below when it has been battened down for a few hours on a hot day. A clean yacht will not smell.

Every few days the bilges will have to be cleaned out and washed down with detergent and disinfectant. At the same time other compartments such as the engine room should get a clean out and all paint and varnish work below decks should be wiped down with a damp cloth. At least once a week all lockers should be emptied and wiped out with a damp cloth. It will be realised that the skipper or mate will have to organise this cleaning chore and everybody has to take his turn at it.

Deck work

At least once a day the deck and cockpit will have to be washed down, usually with salt water and a deck broom. If the yacht is sailing along fast at the time be very careful when collecting water with a bucket on a lanyard from over the side. The pull of the bucket can be severe and can be powerful enough to jerk an unprepared crewman over the side.

If the bucket is dropped upside down a little ahead of the crewman and as it starts to fill is jerked from the water no trouble should be experienced, but care should be taken not to allow the bucket to bang against the paintwork.

When sluicing water around the deck take care not to let it go down open vents, portholes or hatchways: you may soak the skipper down below and he will not be amused.

There is often some brass work to be polished on deck or some brightwork to be cleaned when the decks have been washed and there is bound to be some odd jobs to be done such as lashings to be replaced. The skipper will say what is wanted.

10 Behaviour

Probably the most difficult advice to give in a book for a novice crew is that on how to behave, especially today when there are differing standards between one generation and another. At the same time personal behaviour is of paramount importance when a group of people are cooped up together on a yacht under strange and sometimes unpleasant and frightening conditions. The good crewman must, therefore, take the advice given below in the spirit in which it is offered—as an aid.

The most important and at the same time a very difficult thing to do is to know what one's own peculiarities are, to be able to analyse them in relation to other people, and most difficult of all, to control them so that they are not offensive to others.

Consideration for others

Everyone has their own peculiarities which pass without comment or are unobserved in daily life, but which may get on other people's nerves in the intimate atmosphere of a small boat where privacy is virtually impossible. If you are the only smoker on board, and must light up during or even at the end of a meal it is simple courtesy to ask 'Do you mind if I smoke?' If you are a heavy smoker it is much wiser to smoke on deck. It is the unobtrusive consideration for others that makes for a happy voyage.

Personal cleanliness

It is regrettable that there are the occasional crewmen and sometimes women whose standards of personal cleanliness are not up to that which is necessary when a group of people are living at close quarters below decks in a yacht. It is difficult for even the skipper to make observations on this very personal matter to a new crew member and it is, therefore, advised that every effort should be made not to offend in this way. This does not mean that you should use more than your fair share of the water and washing facilities. With a little care and thought it is possible to keep yourself and your gear quite clean with a surprisingly small amount of water.

Sleeping, eating and drinking habits

If the prospective crewman is a snorer and has not found any way of preventing this habit it can only be advised that he sticks to day sailing. The persistent loud snorer is a menace on a small yacht as he denies all the rest of the crew adequate sleep, and if the yacht is alongside another he may even keep that crew awake also. Other noisy sleepers, the talkers, groaners and splutterers, are acceptable provided they do not cause too much disturbance too frequently.

All that can be advised regarding eating habits is to adapt your table manners to the others. Though the standard of manners today is not so rigid as it was in the past it is very easy to offend, though no one will venture comment or criticism. In this connection make sure that you do not always grab the choicest bits of food or the last piece; a pig is the last thing that is wanted on board.

Again, adapt your drinking habits to what the crew do, at least until you are accepted as one of them. However, unless you are experienced with foreign drinks be careful as they may be stronger than those you are accustomed to. Be especially careful when drinking ashore in the evening as it can be very dangerous to return to a yacht in a small dinghy in a drunken condition. If you are a non-drinker or a light drinker do not think that you will have to drink; this is where the crew's consideration for you comes into play.

Dirty work

There are a number of dirty, irksome, and sometimes exhausting tasks that have to be carried out on yachts. Make sure that you do your fair share, are first to volunteer and do the job without making a fuss about it. Some jobs you will be able to do without being told, so go ahead and do them; you can be sure that the skipper will notice and approve even if he does not mention it.

Obstruction

It is very easy to cause an obstruction on a small yacht just by standing in the companionway (entrance) or sitting in the cockpit or below with your legs obstructing movement. This can be very annoying to others, especially the skipper when he is busy navigating and needs to get from the chart table to the deck and back quickly (57). The cook can also get very annoyed if obstructed when working in the galley.

Make sure that you never sit or stand on ropes, as they may be required in a hurry by other crew members, nor get in the way of them when they are working. By all means help but do not obstruct.

There is usually a favoured seat in the cockpit or in the saloon below and if the sun is shining a choice place on deck. Do not always hog these select places.

Skippers' 'bêtes noires'

Most skippers have some special aversions which would be quite unobjectionable to most people. These are usually tied up with some past event or person and are sometimes quite unreasonable. Try to find out what these are from crewmates who have sailed with him before and endeavour not to offend. It would be unkind to give examples in this book as some are almost unbelievably trivial.

Psychology

There is scope for a separate study on the psychological effects produced by sailing in a small yacht. Rather like intoxicants, it seems to bring out the best and the worst in people. It also tends to exaggerate any special characteristics: a bully becomes more of a bully, the excitable become more so and calm persons calmer. One thing is certain: after a cruise a novice crew will know much more about himself and a surprising amount about his mates.

The best way to find out about anyone is to have them on a small yacht for a week or so. At the end of this period you will have a sound knowledge of their capabilities and characteristics, and most important, their faults and weaknesses.

57   *Do not become a 'companionway pest' by standing or sitting in the companionway, making it difficult for all who want to go below or come up on deck*

The psychological effect of skippering is even more pronounced as skippers have to carry an additional load of responsibility and leadership on their shoulders. Frequently they have to carry out the role of navigator in addition. This combined load is sometimes too much for the occasional skipper, particularly those with little experience, and leads to strange behaviour.

Some skippers when they are overwrought, worried or frightened may be inclined to bellow and shout. Some are not above using streams of flowery language in order to let off steam. Should you be the recipient of one of these outbursts you should not be upset or offended but endeavour to fulfil the skipper's orders to the best of your ability, remembering that the yacht and the responsibility belong to the skipper alone. If you cannot stand such behaviour the cure is in your own hands: do not crew for this person again. Do

121

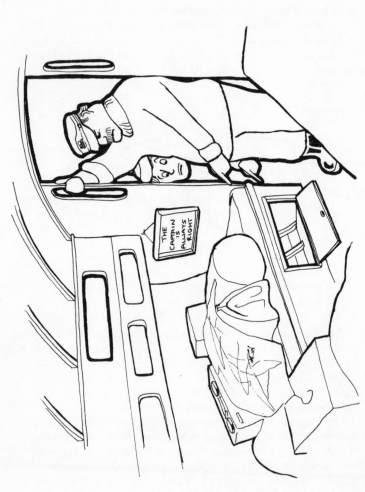

58 *Most people bring on board more gear and clothing than they need. The space allocated for stowage is very limited*

not be put off sailing by one tyrannical skipper but try another; there are many who do not behave in this way.

Most skippers are very sensitive about any damage or threat of damage to their yacht, as they unconsciously consider their yacht an extension of themselves and feel such damage as a direct personal hurt. Their reactions and behaviour are therefore naturally much more violent than one might expect.

Women crew

This book has been written for both men and women crew because more and more women are taking to the sport of sailing. It becomes the exception now to find a yacht which does not have a woman on board. In some ways women are better on a yacht than men. When concentration over a long period is required they can be more reliable and they are often better at staying awake and alert on night watches. Women on the whole keep themselves, the yacht and by example the male members of the crew cleaner. The good crew *man* should realise that good crew *women* have their weaknesses and take them into account. Normally they are not so strong physically and should not be employed where maximum muscle power is needed. They are more sensitive to cold and wet and in dangerous conditions may become more anxious than men. Occasionally they let their emotional commitments to other crew members create unfortunate situations. However, both the virtues and failings of women crew are to be found in men crew.

It is regrettable but at the same time understandable to find that many crewmen look at any woman on a yacht as a stand-in for their mother and expect her to be a galley slave and a general cleaner, tidier-up, washer and repairer. It is up to the skipper and the good crewman to see that she is not unfairly treated. The majority of women go to sea because they want to sail, and do not like being laden with household chores.

11   Other Rigs

So far we have been considering crewing a normal bermudan sloop similar to the great majority of yachts that are to be found today. The novice crew may, however, find himself on board a boat which is a gaff rigged sloop or cutter instead of a bermudan (or marconi rigged) sloop, or even find himself on a yacht with more than one mast, such as a schooner, ketch or yawl, any of which may have either gaff or bermudan rig (61-4). The main characteristics are given in outline below.

Gaff rig

A gaff main is not triangular in shape (as is the bermudan) but has four sides, the upper one attached to a gaff (a spar). This gaff has a throat halyard attached to the end near the mast (the throat) and a peak halyard attached to the outer end of the gaff (the peak). By means of these two halyards the gaff boom is hoisted and the sail with it.

Hoisting

When hoisting it is necessary to keep the gaff boom horizontal until the luff of the sail (the edge nearest the mast) is taut (59). The gaff is then peaked up using the peak halyard, and the two halyards adjusted so that the sail sets correctly and there are no creases or folds in it. The ensign on some yachts is then transferred from the ensign staff to an ensign halyard which runs to the peak of the gaff boom. Points to watch which will be different for each yacht are as follows. If the yacht is rolling watch out for the gaff when the sail ties are removed; it can deliver a nasty bang. See that the mast hoops or lacing attaching the luff of the sail to the mast do not jam on the mast as the sail is hoisted. Make sure that the gaff is hoisted on the correct side of the topping lifts; if there are twin topping lifts the leeward one is usually slacked off first. If there are running backstays the leeward one should be slack and the gaff must also be hoisted on the proper side of these.

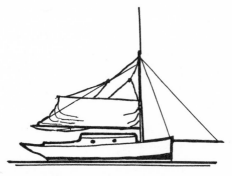

59   *A gaff mainsail is hoisted with the gaff horizontal. During hoisting the gaff must be guided between the topping lifts and running backstays. When the throat is fully hoisted the gaff is then peaked. The two halyards are finally adjusted to remove any creases in the sail*

Handling

The drills once the sail is set are as for a bermudan mainsail except that both halyards have to be paid out at the same time when reefing. When gybing more care is necessary to see that the mainsheets are hauled well in so that the sail gybes under control. An uncontrolled gybe places very considerable strains on the rigging as the heavy gaff swings across. A gaff mainsail has one great advantage over a bermudan sail when coming into harbour in that it can be scandalized by slacking off on the peak halyard until the gaff is horizontal, and on a loose-footed sail, tricing up the tack. This takes all the drive out of the sail. Should extra power be required it is only necessary to peak the sail up again to reset it and get it pulling. This is not effective if the wind is aft of the beam.

Lowering

The preparations for lowering are as for a bermudan main, but if there is an ensign up on the gaff boom it must be lowered first. When lowering a gaff sail the important thing is to keep the gaff under control. A crewman holding the ensign halyard on one side and another on the other side with the topsail sheet (more about this sheet later), both of which run to the peak, will stop the gaff from swinging from side to side. This drill may not be necessary on a small yacht, but some yachts may have vangs rigged for this purpose (60). The crewmen on the two halyards smartly lower the gaff boom in either the peaked or horizontal position without letting the halyards run out of control. A gaff is a nasty thing to drop onto the deck as it can do a lot of damage. When the gaff is on top of the main boom the peak is lashed down to it and the sail furled. This is usually done by pulling the leech along the boom as far forward as possible and then making a bag with the foot of the sail and putting the rest of the sail in it, finally rolling it tight along one side of the boom and lashing it in place. It all sounds more complicated than it is in practice. Get to know the position and function of each rope and it soon ceases to be difficult. Smaller gaff rigged yachts are less complicated.

Topsail

The topsail is a triangular sail that fills the area between the mast and the gaff boom. It is a useful sail as it is easy to hoist and lower under almost any conditions.

The forward side of the sail, the luff, has a series of cringles (eyelets). A rope or wire called a leader, which is attached to the top of the mast, is led through these cringles and the other end attached to the deck close to the mast. This sail is hoisted up the leader by a halyard attached to the head of the sail. The aft corner, the clew, is attached to a sheet which is led through a block on the outer end of the gaff and down to the deck via a block near the throat. Finally the bottom corner of the sail, the tack, has a tackline down to the foot of the mast. All the tackle for the topsail is kept on one side of the mast and inside topping lifts and the other halyards.

60   *In any seaway it is important for a crewman to hold the vangs, ensign halyard or topsail sheet to prevent the gaff swinging about when the mainsail is lowered. The sail can be lowered with the gaff slightly peaked if necessary*

Bowsprit

Most gaff rigged yachts also have a bowsprit from which one or more sails will be set. Some bermudan rigged yachts also have bowsprits. The rigging and drills will vary from one yacht to another, so only an outline is given here (67).

On some older yachts the bowsprit can be a very long spar indeed, whereas those on modern craft are usually short and may be in the form of a platform. The bowsprit is held in position laterally by bowsprit shrouds running from the outer end of the spar to each side of the yacht, and prevented from rising by a bobstay from the end down to about the waterline on the bow. This bobstay may have a tackle so that it can be slacked off and triced up (pulled up) by means of a line and secured out of the way of the anchor chain or mooring line. The fourth stay to the bowsprit end is the topmast stay (or jibstay), which runs to the top of the mast. The bowsprit is stayed in both vertical and lateral directions by this standing rigging.

The staysail is set on the stay that goes from the stem of the yacht (the forward part of the hull) to a point some feet below the top of the mast. The tack of the jib is often secured to a metal ring traveller fitted around the bowsprit that can be hauled out by means of an outhaul line to the bowsprit end. This jib will be set flying (not attached to the stay) if on a traveller from a block just above the point where the forestay joins the mast. Finally a jib topsail can be set in fine weather, from the end of the bowsprit to a block right at the top of the mast. As there is no traveller for this sail a crew member must go out on the end of the bowsprit to tack it in place and assist in hoisting and lowering—a nerve-racking experience the first time.

Topmast

The older gaff rigged boats will have their masts in two pieces. The mainmast has a topmast fitted to the top of it at the hounds (the band and brackets that join the two masts together). It is possible that you may meet one of the now rare yachts that can house its topmast in stormy weather, lowering it by block and tackle so that it is almost as low as the mainmast.

Cutter rig

A cutter is a yacht which has both a forestay and a topmast stay (or jib stay) and sets two or more sails forward of the mast (61). The only problem is in getting a large jib round in front of the forestay when tacking. It is frequently desirable to have a crewman on the foredeck each time to haul this sail forward and pass it in front of the forestay. The mainsail can be either bermudan or gaff rigged.

128

61   *Gaff cutter*

62   *Gaff yawl*

63   *Gaff ketch*

64   *Gaff schooner*

61–4   *The usual rig for a modern yacht is as a bermudan sloop, but cutters, yawls, ketches and schooners are often seen, either bermudan or gaff rigged. There are many other types of rig but they are rare*

Yawls

A yawl, which can have its main mast bermudan or gaff rigged, has a small mizzen mast stepped aft of the sternpost or waterline (62). There are no special problems associated with this rig, but when sailing with a beam wind a mizzen staysail can be set on a stay put up for this purpose from the top of the mizzen mast to near the foot of the mainmast. When tacking or gybing this sail and its stay have to be removed.

Ketches

A ketch is very similar to a yawl except that the mizzen mast and sail is larger and stepped forward of the sternpost (63). There are no special problems with this rig.

Schooners

A schooner is similar to a ketch except that the after mast is larger and stepped amidships so that it becomes the mainmast, and what would be the mainmast is further forward, smaller and called the foremast. The sail on this (shorter) foremast is called the foresail and this is inclined to confuse a novice crew as it is also a name loosely applied to the sail or sails forward of the mast of a single masted vessel. Schooners have one nasty habit in that when the wind is aft of the quarter the foresail can gybe back and forth without warning due to the backwind behind the mainsail, delivering a nasty bang to anyone in the way.

There are many other types of rig but these are rare and are beyond the scope of a book of this nature.

12   Leaving Ship

Customs

As previously mentioned crew must not bring back into the UK customed goods in excess of the duty-free concessions unless they are prepared to pay the custom dues. All goods must be declared on arrival in a UK port when the Customs officer boards, and no one should go ashore until the yacht has been cleared. When going ashore do not take others' customed goods with you as you may be in trouble, since the concessions are personal and are not transferable.

It is vitally important to declare everything that you have brought as if the ship is rummaged (searched) and undeclared goods found, not only will you be in trouble but the skipper is liable to lose his yacht or at least to have it virtually pulled to bits by the rummage crew.

It is hardly necessary to warn crew members that should any attempt be made to smuggle drugs, and this includes 'pot', the most severe penalties are possible. Maritime law is much more severe than civil law.

There has always been an excellent relationship between Customs officers and yachtsmen and it is important to keep this so by all concerned being scrupulously honest.

Leaving ship

All too soon the cruise comes to an end and our good crewman will have to pack and leave. There is one more task still to perform, which is to help clean out the yacht. The crew should not rush off directly the yacht reaches the home port but should allow at least half a day to help in cleaning and restocking.

It is impossible to clean out a yacht with personal gear aboard so he should pack it all up leaving his shore clothing on top of his luggage, while wearing gear suitable for cleaning. Care is necessary to make quite sure that he has collected all his equipment. The number of items that are left on board yachts by crews are legion. All personal gear should be placed on deck, or better still on shore, and the crew, working as a team, get down to a complete cleanout of the yacht, from 'truck to keelson'. If there has been a full crew on board it will be necessary to limit the number working below so that they do not get in each other's way. There may be a final settlement of accounts for food, drink, etc. so ask the skipper or ship's accountant.

When all is completed a change into shore clothes and farewell all round, not forgetting to offer lifts if you are leaving by car. Do not forget a short letter of thanks to the skipper, and should you have taken any photos let him see them as he may like some prints.

One of the delights of yachting as a sport is that the variations are almost unlimited, because each skipper, each yacht, each crew man or woman is different, and together they produce an almost infinite variation of ways in which a yacht can be handled. The author has endeavoured to steer a middle course between the easy-going and the disciplinarian, the slap-happy and the over-cautious, the modern ideas and those of the past, but one thing is quite certain: he will have offended someone by proposing some action with which they do not agree.

The author hopes that this book will have helped any novice crewman going on his first cruise to carry out his duties with pleasure and assurance so that he will thoroughly enjoy himself. Good sailing!

Appendix A Glossary of Nautical Terms

There are a multitude of special nautical terms used by seamen and yachtsmen throughout the ages. These are being added to each year as new materials, designs, methods and equipment are produced. There is a tendency for some people for their self-edification to use these or even more unusual terms without explanation at every available opportunity, creating an aura of 'black magic' of which they alone are master. Do not be put off by this ploy: demand an explanation every time and they will soon tire. The novice should read this glossary through and endeavour to learn those terms italicised. Never be afraid to use basic English such as 'Grab the thick rope at your feet and pull like hell' if the situation and state of knowledge demands it.

Aback   When a vessel is on the starboard tack, the sails are said to be aback when the wind blows on their port-hand surface, and vice versa.

Abaft   Behind, aft of, e.g. abaft the mast—between the mast and the stern.

Abeam   At right angles to the centre of the fore-and-aft line; also abreast, on the beam.

About   see *tacking*.

Abreast   see *abeam*.

Accommodation   The sleeping and domestic arrangements in a hull.

Adrift   Broken away, not under power or control.

Afloat   Waterborne.

Aft   Behind, towards the rear.

After part   The rear part of the vessel.

Aground   On the bottom.

Ahead   Directly in front.

Aldis   A powerful electric signalling lamp.

A'lee   In a leeward direction, e.g. 'Helm a'lee', said when the tiller is put down to leeward.

Aloft   Above deck level.

Amidships   A line across the vessel equidistant from stem and stern.

Antifouling   Paint coating on the bottom of a boat to prevent marine growth or borers. In the tropics copper sheet was traditionally used.

Apeak   The position of a ship when, in weighing the anchor, her cable is 'up and down'.

Apparent wind   The wind on a moving object, and affected by its movement through the air. The faster the boat moves, the more the apparent wind moves ahead.

Arming of lead   Tallow pressed into the hollow in the bottom of a sounding lead to bring up a sample of the seabed.

Astern   Behind the vessel.

Athwart   Across; athwart-hawse—across the stem.

Atrip   The anchor just broken out of the ground.

Avast   Order to stop, e.g. avast heaving.

Awash   With the water washing over.

A'weather   Towards the wind; e.g. 'staysail a'weather', said when the staysail is sheeted on the windward side.

Aweigh   When the anchor is clear of the ground.

Backing (of wind)   When the wind's direction shifts against the sun or anticlockwise, in the N hemisphere.

Backing sails   Hauling the clews of sails to windward, which helps to turn the bow quickly when tacking, or stalls them when heaving to.

Backstays   Standing rigging from the masthead to the stern or quarters of a vessel to take the forward strain on the mast.

Baggywrinkle   Traditional anti-chafe gear made of rope yarn and wrapped round the rigging.

Bail   To remove the water from a boat with an open container.

Ballast   Weight placed in a ship to counterbalance the heeling, to give stiffness.

Bar   A shoal formed across the mouth of a harbour or river by the combined action of stream and current.

Bare poles   Having no sails set.

Batten down   To secure all hatches, lights, etc.

Battens   Light pieces of wood in pockets across the sails to keep them to a designed shape.

Beacon   A guiding light or mark to assist navigation.

Beam   A transverse timber which supports the deck.

Beam   The width of a ship at her widest part.

Beam ends   Of a ship flung completely on her side.

Bear away   To avoid or move away from.

Bear down on   To move directly towards.

Bearing   Direction in degrees referred to the fore-and-aft line of a ship (e.g. on the bow) or to the compass meridian.

Bear off   To shove or steer away; to steer further away from the wind's direction.

Bear up   To keep or move towards the wind.

Beating   To make to windward (see *tacking*).

Beaufort scale   A numerical notation of wind force. See the various winds, e.g. light airs, gale, etc.

Becket   A loop or eye, in rope or wire or on a block.

Before   In front of, e.g. before the mast.

Belay   To secure a rope with figure-of-eight turns round a belaying pin, cleat or bollard.

Belaying pin   A movable pin of metal or wood through a rail or bar, and about which a rope is secured.

Bells   Time on board ship is announced by the strokes of a bell.

Belly   The arching of a sail; also the curved part of a sail.

Bend   To secure one thing to another. A type of knot to join ropes together.

Beneaped   A vessel that is run aground at high water when the tides are working from springs towards neaps, so the next tide fails to float her.

Bermuda or bermudan rig   A triangular mainsail hoisted to the masthead and having a pointed top, with no additional spars near the head. Sometimes called Marconi rig.

Bight   An unknotted loop in a rope; also refers to any part of a rope between its ends.

Bilge   That curve of the underbody on which a boat rests when taking the ground, the main curve between side and bottom. Also the lower interior of the hull.

Binnacle   The housing of the mariner's compass.

Bites (of an anchor)   When it takes hold in the bottom.

Bitts   Strong upright posts through the upper deck of a vessel with a crosspiece connecting them. Used for securing cables, etc.

Block   A pulley. Wood, metal or plastic with internal wheels and external connections, to lead ropes or wires.

Bluff   Steep-to; wide-bowed (of a vessel).

Boat hook   Staff with a hook at one end for picking up moorings or floating objects.

Bobstay   A stay from the stem near the waterline to the bowsprit end, which prevents the bowsprit from lifting.

Bollard   A short heavy iron, stone or wood post on a ship or jetty to which ropes may be secured.

Boltropes   The roping sewn round the edges of sails.

Boom   A spar used to extend the lower part of a sail. It takes its name from the sail it extends, e.g. main boom.

Boomkin (bumpkin)   A small spar, projecting from the ship's side or stern to give a fair lead for sheets or standing rigging.

Boot-topping   A line of specially hard paint round the waterline which can be scrubbed without damage. Less used nowadays since modern antifouling can be scrubbed, but boats with high topsides often look better with boot-topping carried up a little way to reduce the apparent height of topsides.

Bosun's chair   A seat in which a man can be hoisted aloft. The best are made of canvas, but if a wooden one like a swing seat is used the ropes must pass right underneath the seat, so that if the wood breaks the occupant is still supported by the rope.

Bottle screw   An adjusting screw fitted to the bottom of wire rigging. Cruisers usually use open ones, more correctly called rigging screws, on which the threads can be more easily inspected. Also called a turnbuckle.

Bottom   The underwater body of a ship.

Bower   The principal anchor, carried in the bow.

Bows   The sides of the forward part of the ship.

Bowse   To haul or tighten.

Bowsprit   The spar projecting forward from the stem.

Break   To break out; to wrench an anchor from its hold in the bottom.

Breast rope   A short line leading from a boat across to the quayside or another boat alongside, and running at right angles to the boat, rather than off at an angle.

Bridle   A rope, chain or wire used for connecting two objects.

Bridge deck   Reinforcing beams and bulkheads, decked over, between the cockpit and the cabin. Strengthens boat a great deal and also prevents much water going down the companionway in bad weather, but restricts entrance to the cabin.

Bring to   To stop the ship; to take turns with cables round a capstan.

Bring up   To come to anchor.

Broach to   To swing suddenly into the trough of a sea broadside on. In a small boat, to be carried on the forward side of a big sea with the stern high and the bow depressed until the bow is driven to one side and the boat thrown over on its side.

Broad reach   With wind abaft the beam, between reaching and running.

Broadside   The topsides between bow and quarter.

Brought by the lee   When the wind shifts from one quarter to the other while running. Also called running by the lee.

Bulkheads   Partitions dividing the ship into several compartments.

Bull rope   A rope led from the ring of a mooring buoy inboard through a block at the bowsprit end to haul the buoy clear of the stem.

Bulldog clip   A U-shaped bar with threaded ends carrying nuts and a fairing piece by which an eye or join can quickly be made in wire.

Bullseye   A hardwood round thimble.

Bulwarks   Ship's sides above deck level.

Bunk   A bed-place on board.

Bunkboards   Boards to retain the occupant in a bunk in a seaway. They are often made of canvas, coming much higher than ordinary wooden bunkboard, with lanyards up to eyes in the deckhead. Sometimes wrongly called leeboards.

Buoy   An anchored float indicating a navigational position.

Buoy, mooring   A buoy to the ground tackle to which a ship may be moored.

Buoyancy bags   Airtight bags fitted in dinghies in place of built-in tanks to give buoyancy if waterlogged.

Burgee   A swallow-tailed signal flag; also a triangular distinguishing flag denoting membership of a yacht club.

By the board   Over the side.

By the head   A vessel trimmed to be deeper forward than aft.

By the lee   see *brought by the lee*.

By the stern   Opposite of *by the head*.

By the wind   When a ship is sailing as close to the wind as possible. Also closehauled or on the wind.

Cable   As a measure of distance, 200 yards (100 fathoms), i.e. about one-tenth of a nautical mile.

Cable   The rope or chain of an anchor; a stout, thick rope.

Capstan   A machine for hauling on cable.

Capsize   Overturn, upset.

Careen   To heel a vessel over in order to get at her bottom.

Carry away   To break or part.

Carry way   To continue to move through the water.

Carvel   Method of building a boat with planks edge to edge to present a smooth surface.

Cast off   To disconnect a line. It does not mean let it trail in the water, where it may get entangled with the screws.

Cat   Concerned with weighing and lifting of an anchor, e.g. cathead, cat davit, cat pennant, cat purchase.

Catamaran   Twin-hulled vessel.

Cat's paw   In a period of calm, a local temporary roughening of the surface; a twisting of a rope into two loops through which a block may be hooked.

Caulk   To drive oakum into the seams between planks.

Centreboard (centreplate, drop keel, dagger plate)   A fin of wood or metal which can be lowered through the bottom of a boat to diminish leeway and heeling.

Chainplates (channel plates)   Side fittings taking the lower end of the shrouds.

Chart   A mariner's map.

Charter   To hire a boat or let a boat out for hire.

Check   Of a cable, to stop progress. Of a sheet or halyard, to ease out a little and very slowly.

Chock-a-block (block and block, or two blocks)   When the two blocks of a tackle come together.

Clap on   To man a fall.

Claw off   To work to windward off a lee shore.

Claw ring   A device for attaching the sheet block to a roller reefing boom, forward of the end and rolling on top of the canvas if the sail is reefed.

Claw to windward   To work slowly to windward.

Clean full   Sailing with the wind just freer than closehauled. Also full and by.

Cleat   A two-armed hook of wood or metal to which ropes may be secured.

Clew   The corner at the junction of leech and foot of a sail to which sheets are attached.

Clinker (clincher, clencher)   Method of building in which each side plank overlaps the one below.

Closehauled   Sailing as close to the wind as possible with all sails drawing.

Close-reefed   With all reefs pulled down.

Coachroof   Part of the deck raised to give extra headroom below.

Coaming   The lip round a deck or bulkhead opening to prevent passage of water.

Cockpit   The lower part of a yacht's well, normally the steering position.

Compass   A navigational instrument which indicates a north point and bearings from it.

Composite   A method of construction, employing an iron frame and a wooden skin.

Con   To direct the helmsman.

Constant bearing   When the relative bearing of another vessel does not alter there is risk of collision.

Counter   The projection of a hull abaft the waterline.

Course   The angle made by a ship's track and a meridian.

Cradle   A frame which holds a vessel upright when out of the water.

Crane   A metal projection from the masthead to give a lead to a throat purchase or halyards.

Crane lines   Short tie-backs, usually elastic, used to stop rigging tapping against mast.

Cranse iron   The iron ring at the end of the bowsprit.

Cringles   Eyelets worked into the roping of a sail, e.g. reef cringle, tack cringle.

Crown   The point at which the arms of an anchor join the shank.

Crutch   A trestle for supporting the boom.

Cutter   A single masted fore-and-aft rigged yacht carrying more than one headsail.

Davits   Cranes for lowering and lifting boats.

Dead reckoning   The calculation of the position of a ship, based on her course, speed and taking into consideration the influence of wind and current.

Deck   A horizontal partition of a boat.

Deckhead   The underside of a deck.

Deep   An unmarked graduation of the hand lead line; an area of deep water between stretches of shoals, e.g. Hurd Deep or Barrow Deep.

Deviation   The amount a compass needle deviates east or west from the magnetic meridian due to the influence of iron in the ship.

Diagonal build   A flush double-skinned boat with planks laid diagonally.

Dinghy   A small open boat, may be a tender to a yacht.

Dip   To lower and rehoist a flag in salute.

Displacement   The amount of water displaced by the underwater volume of vessel, and equal to the total weight of vessel and contents. Usually measured in tons or metric tons.

Distress   Need for assistance.

Dodgers   Canvas rigged on the lifelines to help shelter the cockpit.

Doghouse   Raised section at aft end of cabin.

Dog vane   A wisp of bunting in the weather rigging, sometimes called a telltale.

Dolphin   A mooring staging not connected with the shore.

Downhaul   A rope for hauling anything down.

Down helm   To put the tiller to leeward, i.e. downwind.

Dowse   To take in sail or lower spars quickly.

Draught   The maximum underwater depth of the ship.

Draw   Of sails, to fill.

Dress ship   To display flags all over the rigging for decorative purposes.

Drift   The rate of current in knots; the unassisted movement of a ship. See *leeway*.

Drudge   Process of dragging an anchor at short stay along the bottom to give steerage way in a tideway.

Earings   Ropes for securing the clew of a sail to a spar.

Ease   Of a rope, check; of a ship, to luff for a dangerous sea or gust of wind.

Ebb   The falling of the tide from high to low water.

Echo sounder   An electronic device that indicates the depth of water by measuring the time sound waves take to go to the seabed and return.

140

Eddy   A local circular or spiral movement of air or water unrelated to the movement of the surrounding current.

Ensign   A flag carried by a ship to indicate nationality.

Even keel   Level trim, not by the head or by the stern.

Eyes of her   The extreme fore end of a vessel.

Fairleads   Metal channels to prevent chafe and to guide the lead (angle) of a rope.

Fairway   A navigable channel.

Fall   The hauling part of a rope.

Falling off the wind   Paying off to leeward, turning away from the wind.

False keel   A piece of timber bolted to the outside of the main keel.

Fathom   A unit of measurement of depth or length (six feet).

Fend   To push off.

Fenders (fendoffs)   Cushions or pads to protect a ship's side from chafe or bumping.

Fetch   To make or reach a point steered for.

Fid   A tapered piece of wood or iron used to limit the travel of a spar (bowsprit); also used to enlarge holes in rope, canvas, wood or iron.

Fiddle   A bar of wood or metal fitted with a number of small sheaves to provide leads for light running gear.

Fiddle block   A pulley having two sheaves end to end, the upper larger than the lower.

Fife-rail   A rail of wood or metal containing a number of belaying pins.

Fish   To support or strengthen a spar with lashed splints.

Fitting out   The yearly overhaul and spring-clean of a vessel before the start of the sailing season.

Fix   A cross-check which gives one an exact knowledge of a boat's position, derived from two or more position lines.

Flake   One circle of a coil of rope.

Flake, to   To coil a rope down in layers clear for running.

Flare   The concave upward curve of a vessel's bow; a flare-up light signal.

Flat aback   With the wind on the wrong side of the sails.

Flatten in   To haul in the sheets.

Flood   The movement of the tide between low water and high water.

Floors   Athwartship pieces of wood or metal connecting the heels of the ship's frames or timbers (ribs).

Fly   The horizontal measurement of a flag.

Flying   When the luff of a sail, when set, is not hanked to a stay.

Foot   The lower edge of a sail.

Fore   Forward

Fore-reaching   Movement in a boat under sail dead into the eye of the wind when going about, luffing or hove to.

Foresail   The principal sail set on the foremast.

Forge   To move rapidly.

Forward   On the fore side.

Foul anchor   A turn of the cable round an anchor, or an anchor caught upon anything.

Foul berth   At anchor with insufficient swinging room.

Foul bottom   Uneven, rocky patches on the sea bed (foul ground). An underbody coated with weeds or barnacles.

Foul hawse   Crossed or twisted cables.

Founder   To sink.

Frapping   Binding. Also halyards banging on a mast.

Free   Between closehauled and having the wind aft.

Freeboard   The height of the deck from the waterline.

Freshen the nip   To slacken a rope off, to change the position of chafe; of wind, to increase.

Full   A sail which is drawing well.

Full and by   Sailing as close to the wind as possible yet with every sail full and pulling.

Furl   To gather a sail up and secure it to its spar.

Gaff   A boom which extends the head of a four-sided fore-and-aft sail.

Gale   Forces 8 and 9 on the Beaufort scale. A wind of 34–47 knots.

Galley   The kitchen of a ship.

Gallows, permanent   A fixed frame for supporting a boom (see *crutch*).

Gammoning   The fastenings of a bowsprit at the stem.

Gangplank   A board used as a bridge from a ship to a jetty.

Gangway   A passage. The removable part of the bulwarks through which a ship may be boarded.

Gash bin   The ship's dustbin, usually a bucket.

Gather way   To begin to move through the water.

Gear   Used to describe all the tackle of the mast or sail and the steering apparatus. Also a general term for the crew's clothing, bedding, etc.

Genoa   Large triangular headsail for use in lighter winds.

Gimbals   A system of bearings and rings to maintain an article in the horizontal plane at sea.

Gooseneck   A hinged metal fitting used to secure a spar to its mast while allowing it to swing or rise.

Goosewinged   Running before the wind with sails set on opposite sides of the mast.

Grating   A cross-wood framework.

Gripes   Canvas or webbing bands used to secure a boat in davits.

Grommet   An endless ring of rope.

Gudgeons   Ring-shaped sockets on the hull through which the pintles on the rudder pass, and in which they pivot.

Gunter   A triangular mainsail the head of which is extended above the masthead by a vertical yard which slides on the mast.

Gunwale   The upper edge of a boat's side.

Guy   A controlling rope, usually on a spar.

Gybe   When sailing, to bring the wind from one quarter to the other across the stern in such a way that the boom swings across.

Halyard   A rope used for hoisting anything.

Hambro line   A small line used for seizing.

Hand-bearing compass   Portable hand compass fitted with a prism through which bearings of objects may be read.

Hand sheets and halyards   Keeping sheets fast in the hand instead of belaying them when sailing an open boat in squally weather.

Hand   To lower and furl; of a patent log, to bring inboard.

Handspike   A bar of wood used as a lever for raising heavy objects.

Handsomely   Gently or gradually.

Handy-billy   A small tackle; a purchase having a fixed double block fitted with a tail and a moving single block.

Hanks   Rings or clips of metal or plastic seized to headsail luffs to attach them to stays.

143

Hard   A hard area, natural or artificial, on a soft shore.

Hard-a-port, hard-a-starboard   The order to use the maximum effective helm (35°) to make the ship's head go in the direction indicated by the order.

Harden   Of a wind, when a stiff breeze ceases to be gusty.

Harden in   To flatten sails by pulling in their sheets.

Hatchway   An opening with a movable cover (hatch) in the deck of a vessel.

Haul   To pull on a rope.

Haul your wind   To sail closer to the wind.

Hawse   The distance between the stem of a vessel and the holding flukes of the anchor to which she is riding.

Hawse, clear   When riding to two anchors a ship is said to have a clear hawse when one cable has not fouled the other.

Hawse, foul   A ship riding to two anchors with the cables crossed once or more.

Hawsepipes   The holes in the bows of a ship through which the anchor cable runs.

Hawser   A large rope or cable of rope or steel.

Head   The fore end of the ship.

Head of a sail   The upper corner, or hoist.

Heads   The marine toilet, so called because it was traditionally right up in the bow (or head) of the ship.

Headsails   The sails forward of the foremast.

Heave   To haul, to throw.

Heave in sight   To come in view.

Heave short   To shorten in the cable, to 'short stay'.

Heave to   To stop; to take way off; to keep closely head-on to a heavy sea at minimum speed.

Heaving line   Light line, usually with a weight at one end, thrown to make contact between a vessel and the shore when going alongside, etc. A heavier rope can be attached and pulled after it.

Heel   The after end of the keel; the butt of a mast; the sideways inclination of a ship.

Helm   The tiller or wheel.

Helm down   The opposite to helm up; also helm a'lee. To move the tiller away from the wind so that the vessel's head moves towards the wind.

Helm up   To move the tiller (up) towards the wind so that the ship's head goes to leeward; also helm a'weather.

Hitch   To make a rope fast to an object, not to another rope.

Hoist to   To haul aloft. Also the top corner of a triangular sail.

Home sheets   To haul in sheets hard.

Hoops   Rings holding the luff of a sail to a mast.

Horse   A bar, rail or wire running athwartships across a vessel's deck on which a sheet block travels.

Hounds   Projections which support the trestletrees of a mast; that part of the mast from which the upper end of the lower standing rigging is set up.

House flag   A personal pennant.

Housing   The part of a mast or bowsprit inboard; of a topmast, to lower but not strike.

Hug   To keep close to.

Hull   The body of a vessel, not including her masts and fittings.

Hurricane   A Force 12 wind on the Beaufort scale, i.e. about 65 mph.

Iron-bound   Off a rocky coast, where no anchorage is possible.

Irons, in   A ship is in irons when she is head to wind and unwilling to pay off on either tack.

Jacob's ladder   A rope ladder having wooden rungs.

Jaws   The fork at the mast end of a boom or gaff which bears against the mast.

Jib   The foremost headsail; gear appertaining to the jib, e.g. jib sheets.

Jib-boom   An extension of the bowsprit on which additional headsails are set, not the spar at the foot of a jib.

Joggle   To join timber or metal together with a notched projection to prevent the two pieces from sliding.

Joggle-shackle   A long-jawed shackle used in cable work.

Jumper struts   Spreaders that are angled forward so that they give support fore and aft as well as sideways. The stays running over them are known as jumper stays.

Junk   Old rope

Jury   Makeshift, temporary.

Kedge   A small anchor.

Kedge, to   To move a vessel by hauling on a kedge anchor.

Keel   The lowest fore-and-aft member of a vessel.

145

Keep her away   To keep a vessel's head more away from the wind.

Ketch   A two-masted vessel with the after mast (mizzen) shorter than the mainmast and stepped forward of the sternpost.

Kicking strap   A line or tackle rove from a short way along the boom to the heel of the mast, to prevent the boom rising. Makes a boat go faster by keeping the whole of the mainsail nearly in the same plane when the mainsheet is eased, preventing twist.

Killick   A stone used for anchoring on a foul bottom; colloquially, an anchor.

Kink   A sharp and unnatural bend in rope or wire.

Knot   A nautical mile per hour; not now used as a measure of distance.

Labour   The violent movement of a vessel in a seaway.

Lacing   A line securing a sail to its spar.

Laid up   Unrigged and dismantled.

Lanyard   Lashing, short piece of line or cord.

Lash   To secure wth ropes.

Latitude   Measurement north or south of the Equator.

Launch   To allow to slip into the water.

Lay   Of a rope, the direction left or right in which the strands of a rope or hawser are twisted; also to 'lay aft'—to go aft; to put.

Laying-up   Storing a boat for the winter, afloat, in a mud berth or ashore.

Lay off a course   To draw on a chart.

Lazy   Extra, e.g. lazy guy, lazy painter.

Lead   A leaden weight on the end of a marked line (lead line) used to ascertain the depth of water.

Lead   The trend or angle of a rope or something which directs it.

Leading edge   The forward edge of any moving object such as a rudder, centreboard or aircraft wing. The leading edge of a sail is the luff.

Lee   The side away from the wind.

Leeboards   Boards pivoted on the sides of shallow draught vessels which, when lowered, increase the resistance to making leeway. Wrongly used to refer to a board or canvas on the inboard edge of a bunk.

Lee-bowing   Sailing a boat against the tide in such a way that the tide is on the lee bow instead of the weather bow, thereby

146

pushing the boat up to windward. If a slight degree of pinching brings the tide on the lee bow instead of the weather bow, it is worth doing.

Lee-going tide   A tidal stream which sets with the direction of the wind.

Lee-ho   A warning that the helm has been put down for going about and that the vessel is coming head to wind.

Leech   The after edge of a sail. On a squaresail, the vertical edges.

Leeward   Down wind.

Leeway   The angle between the ship's fore-and-aft line and her wake. The wind causes the vessel to move slightly sideways as she sails along.

Leg   A tack.

Legs   Stout baulks of timber, their upper ends bolted to the outside of a vessel through midship timbers near the sheer-strake and guyed fore-and-aft in vertical position, to support the boat in an upright position when laid ashore (drying out ashore).

Let draw   To permit a sail to fill on the desired tack.

Let fly   Let go sheets.

Let go   Of an anchor, to let it fall into the water.

Lie over   (see *heel*)

Lifeline   A stout line rigged about the deck to provide handhold for the crew.

Lifebelt   Circular or horseshoe-shaped float, kapok, foam plastic or cork-filled and usually big enough to encircle a man's chest.

Lift   A rope to take the weight of a spar.

Light airs   Forces 1 and 2 Beaufort scale; wind of 1–6 nautical miles per hour.

Light breeze   Force 3 Beaufort scale; wind 7–10 nautical miles per hour.

Limbers   Holes in the floors and between the timbers (ribs) and hull to permit the free passage fore and aft of bilge water.

Lines, heaving   Light lines weighted at one end and used for throwing to pass the end of a hawser.

List   The inclination of a vessel from the horizontal due to a transverse change in trim.

Lizard   A short length of rope with a thimble or eye fitted in one end.

LOA   Length overall of a boat, i.e. the length of the hull, but not including any spars outboard such as bowsprit or bumpkin.

Locker   Cupboard.

Log   A contrivance by which the speed of a vessel is estimated.

Logbook, log   A ship's diary.

Longitude   Measurement east or west in degrees of the prime meridian of Greenwich.

Loom   The handle of an oar. Also the glow in the sky of a light, sometimes visible before the light itself.

Lubber's point or lubber line   A fixed mark beside or inside a compass bowl indicating the direction of the ship's head.

Luff   Of a sail, its leading or weather edge.

Luff, to   To bring a vessel closer to the wind.

Luff tackle   A working tackle with a double and a single block.

Lug   A projection.

LWL   Load water line of vessel—a line to which she floats when at her designed weight. It is a basic characteristic of a vessel because boat's speed is related to waterline length through the drag caused by the waves built up. The maximum speed of a boat that cannot plane is the square root of the effective waterline length, multiplied by about 1·2.

Make   To reach (e.g. to make port); of tides, the increase of the tidal range and velocity from neaps to springs.

Make a sternboard   To make a vessel go astern under sail.

Make sail   To set the sails.

Make water   To leak.

Making way   Moving ahead or astern through the water. Not to be confused with 'under way'.

Man   To provide an adequate crew; (of a fall, see *clap on*).

Marks   Graduations of the hand lead line which reveal the depth by sight or touch.

Marl   To take a number of turns of line round anything, each turn concluding with a half-knot.

Marline   Light, two-stranded line, suitable for marling.

Marlinespike, marling spike   A tapered wood or steel tool for opening up the strands of rope or wire.

Marry   To join unlayed rope ends together strand for strand; of ropes and falls, to hold two ropes together in order to haul on both equally.

Mast A spar or system of pieces of wood or metal placed nearly perpendicular to the keel of a boat and used to support other spars on which sails are spread.

Mast step A socket in the keelson in which the mast heel is set up or stepped. May also be placed on deck.

Maul A large hammer.

Meridian A true north and south line.

Messenger A small rope bent onto a large one and brought to a capstan in order to heave the larger one in when by itself it is too big to be brought up.

Midships Of the helm, the executive order to centre the rudder. (see *amidships*.)

Mile A nautical mile is equal to one minute of latitude at the Equator, and is universally accepted as being 6,080 feet.

Miss stays To hang up in the wind and fail to come about and pay off on a new tack, when tacking.

Mizzen mast The after mast in vessels such as ketches and yawls.

Mizzen sails Sails set from mizzen mast.

Moor To lie to more than one anchor; to pick up a mooring.

Moored all fours Moored between anchors or cables from both bows and both quarters.

Mooring, double Permanent mooring with a mooring chain shackled to the centre of a heavy ground chain stretched between two anchors or clumps.

Mooring, single Permanent mooring with one anchor or clump.

Moorings Permanent anchors, heavy weights, etc. laid down in the bed of a harbour, to which a mooring chain is shackled. The mooring chain is hauled inboard and bitted by a vessel picking up the mooring. It is pulled up on a length of rope (a buoy rope), and its position is indicated by a mooring buoy. To slip a mooring is to let it go, casting the buoy adrift.

Mouse A knob or thickening worked on a rope with spunyarn, etc. generally to form a neat stop to prevent the rope from overhauling through a block, etc.

Mouse, to To take several turns with yarn round the back and bill of a hook to prevent it jerking out of its hold.

Multihull Vessel with more than one hull.

Nail sickness Minor leaks in a ship's side by the galvanic action of seawater on bare iron fastenings, nails, etc. The fastenings erode, leaving unplugged nail holes, through which the water percolates.

Navel pipes   Metal lined openings in the deck through which the anchor cable runs from the chain locker.

Navigation   The art of conducting a vessel in safety from one point to another.

Neaped or beneaped   Left aground by a receding spring tide, so that the succeeding tide will be insufficient to refloat the vessel.

Neaps   The tides with the least rise and fall, having the lowest high water and highest low water of the tide cycle; i.e. having the least range.

Nip   The point at which a rope or cable bends sharply, e.g. round a cleat, block or pin, or (of a cable) over the lip of a hawsepipe or fairlead.

Nip, to   Of a hawser, etc. to make it fast with a seizing.

Nip, freshen the   To move a rope or wire such as a halyard so that a different part takes the heavy load and wringing effect at a sheave.

Nothing off   An order to the helmsman not to let the vessel fall off the wind.

Off   Offshore, e.g. the wind taking off, blowing offshore; near to, e.g. anchored off Ryde; away from, e.g. off the wind.

Off and on, to stand   To keep close to the land, but alternately closing with and then withdrawing from the shore.

Offing   The open sea at a safe distance from the shore; the open sea viewed from the security of a sheltered anchorage during a gale.

Off the wind   Sailing on any point other than closehauled.

On   Opposite to off; towards, e.g. a wind blowing onshore.

On the wind   Closehauled.

On end   Upright or vertical; of a mast, set up and secured in position.

Open   Undecked; of an anchorage, unsheltered.

Open hawse   Riding to two bower anchors without a swivel.

Out   Away from the shore.

Outboard   Beyond the ship's sides or ends.

Outhaul   A rope used to haul anything out into position, e.g. a clew outhaul.

Overcast   Cloud-covered sky.

Overfall Tide rip; effect of shoal.

Overhaul To gain on; of a rope, to slacken off; of a tackle, to draw the blocks apart—opposite to fleeting; of gear, to examine and make ready.

Painter A rope attached to the stem ringbolt of a small boat, and used for securing the boat to anything.

Palm A form of thimble which straps across the palm of the hand, and is used by sailmakers when roping or seaming canvas; the flat face of an anchor fluke.

Parallel rules Rules, used in navigation for transferring bearings on a chart, designed so that they can be moved around on a chart with the edges always parallel.

Parcel To wind overlapping strips of canvas tightly round a rope with its lay. To bind a mooring hawser with turns of rope, canvas or junk in order to prevent chafe at a point where it passes through a fairlead.

Parrel A ring for keeping a spar close to its mast.

Parrel balls Hardwood beads on a parrel to give it a frictionless travelling and turning surface.

Parrel line The piece of rope or wire on which the parrel balls are threaded, and which secures them to the parrel.

Part Of a rope; e.g. standing part, running part, hauling part.

Part, to To break or carry away.

Partners The supporting timbers where a mast passes through the deck.

Pay down To pass cables or hawsers below decks.

Pay off To allow a ship's head to swing away from the wind.

Pay out To slacken a rope hand over hand and while controlling it.

Peak The outer end of a gaff, also the sail at the gaff end. The narrowest part at either end of a ship's interior.

Peak, to To set up on a gaff sail's peak halyard, until wrinkles begin to appear in the throat of the sail.

Peg to windward To make good to windward under difficulties.

Pennant or pendant A short piece of rope or wire, one end of which, the standing out end, is made fast to a spar or sail. In the other end is an eye to hold the hook or the upper block of a tackle. A triangular flag.

Pig A cast piece of ballast.

Pin   The axle of the sheave of a block. Also belaying pin.

Pinching   Sailing very close to the wind, with some loss of speed.

Pintles   Metal pins on a rudder which pivot in the gudgeons.

Plate   Metal fittings at a ship's sides to which the lower ends of the shrouds, backstays, runners, etc. are set up. Also centre-board.

Plug   The stopper for the draining hole in the bottom of a boat.

Point   One thirty-second part of a circle, i.e. 11° 15′.

Pointing   A degree of closeness to the wind at which a vessel will sail full and by.

Points, cardinal   The four main compass points: north, south, east and west.

Points, reef   Cords on either side of a reef band, used to tie up the unwanted foot of the sail when reefed.

Pooped, to be   When in running before a heavy sea the seas overtake the vessel and fall on board the after part.

Popple   A short, confused sea.

Port   On the left hand side facing forward.

Port tack   With the wind blowing on the port side.

Pram   A Norwegian pattern dinghy, with a small transom rather than a point at the bow.

Preventer   An additional stay set up to counteract the bending strain of a spar, or to prevent sudden movement.

Pulpit   A strong rail around the bow of a yacht above the deck.

Punt   Colloquial name for a small flat-bottomed dinghy.

Purchase   A system of blocks to increase hauling power.

Pushpit   A structure of tubing similar to a pulpit, but in the stern of a boat. Its object is to prevent people falling overboard. Stern pulpit.

Put back   Return.

Quarter   Midway between the beam and right aft.

Quarter berth   A bunk running under the side of the cockpit.

Race   Locally disturbed water due to currents, streams, wind and shoals.

Rack   Stowage space.

Rack   To seize together with racking seizing round two ropes, one of which is subject to more strain than the other.

Rake   The inclination of a vessel's mast in the fore-and-aft line.

Range   Of cable, to flake down on deck in large bights. Of tide, the difference between the rise and fall of any given tide.

Reach   To sail with the wind free.

Ready about   The warning of the helmsman's intention to tack.

Reef   To shorten sail.

Reef, Spanish   To tie a knot in the canvas of a headsail.

Reeve   To thread or pass a rope through anything.

Relieving tackles   Temporary tackles set up to the steering gear to assist the helmsman in heavy weather.

Render   To give; to yield; to operate freely.

Rhumb line   The shortest distance between two points, a straight line on a Mercator chart; a course cutting all meridians at the same angle.

Ride   To be at anchor or moorings.

Riding light   All-round white light shown when at anchor.

Rig   The arrangement of a ship's masts, rigging and sails.

Rig, to   To set up.

Roach   A curved edge to a sail.

Rocket   A distress signal.

Roll   Transverse motion on a vessel.

Roller reefing   A method of reefing in which the sail is rolled up round a revolving boom.

Round in   To haul in quickly and steadily.

Round turn   One complete turn round anything.

Roundly   Quickly and steadily (opposite to handsomely).

Rowlocks   Square gaps in the gunwale of a boat to act as fulcrums for the oars. Also frequently misused for metal or plastic crutches for oars (oarlocks).

Rubbing strake   An additional thick piece of wood, running the length of a boat and made fast on the outside of the planking a short distance below the gunwale, to protect the boat from damage when lying alongside.

Rudder   A flat plate hinged to the sternpost and used to direct the movement of the ship.

Runner   The purchase bowsing down the lower end of a running backstay. Also the running backstays, detached when likely to obstruct the boom.

Running   Sailing with the wind right aft.

Saloon   Main living space in a vessel.

Samson post Stout post mounted on stem or keelson, coming through the deck for attaching anchor cable or mooring lines. Deck beams should be well reinforced in way of the samson post.

Scandalize To trice up the tack and lower the peak of a gaff sail. Spills wind and is quicker than reefing.

Scend The lift of the bows of a boat to the sea or swell. Also refers to large waves finding their way into harbour.

Schooner A fore-and-aft rigged vessel with two or more principal masts, of which the foremost is shorter.

Scope The length of cable by which a vessel is anchored.

Scuppers Apertures in the bulwarks to permit water to run off the deck.

Scuttle To sink a vessel deliberately. A glazed aperture to admit light and air.

Sea anchor Canvas drogue to reduce a boat's speed through the water or hold it head-on to wind and sea.

Seacock Valves for shutting off pipes which pass through the hull.

Seize To fasten two things together with turns of line round both (seizings).

Semaphore A method of signalling with two arms, used by persons or signal stations.

Serve To bind a line tightly round a rope against the lay.

Set a course To steer a given course.

Set flying A jib (or mizzen staysail, which is often set flying) attached only to its halyard and sheet and tack downhaul, not hanked to a stay.

Set up To rig; to hoist a sail; to tighten lanyards or shrouds; to flatten sails.

Settle To lower a sail a little and handsomely; of a ship, to sink slowly.

Sextant An instrument used in navigation for measuring horizontal angles between objects or vertical angles of heavenly bodies.

Shackle An iron fitting, D-shaped, U-shaped, saddle shaped, bow-shaped, etc. the open (clear) end of which may be closed by a pin; used for connecting objects.

Shank The shaft of an anchor.

Sheave The wheel of a block on which the rope runs.

Sheer   The fore-and-aft curve of a vessel's deckline.

Sheer, to   To move across.

Sheerstrake   The topmost plank of a ship's side.

Sheet anchor   A spare bow anchor, an invaluable standby.

Sheets   A rope or ropes controlling the clew of a sail.

Shift   To change clothes, sails; to alter the position of something.

Ship   To take anything on board.

Shoal   Shallow.

Shore   To buttress up.

Shrouds   Lateral stays to the mast.

Skin   The outer planking of a vessel.

Slack in stays   Sluggish in going about.

Slack water   When the tidal stream is stationary.

Slant   Wind in a favourable position.

Slew   To swing round.

Snatch block   A block, the side of which is cut away or hinged to allow a bight of line to be 'snatched' round the sheave.

Snub   To check suddenly.

Soldier's wind, with a   There and back without tacking.

Sound   To ascertain the depth.

Spar   A piece of timber on which a sail is set.

Spell   An interval. Also to relieve someone from his task.

Spent   Broken or finished.

Spill wind   To empty a sail of wind.

Spinnaker   A light weather triangular sail boomed out from the mast on the opposite side to the mainsail.

Splice   To join by interweaving strands of rope or wire.

Springs   The tides having the maximum range in a tide cycle. Mooring ropes leading from forward in the boat to a jetty bollard farther aft, or from aft to a point ashore farther forward.

Stanchion   A supporting column or pillar. Also the supports for wire lifelines around the deck.

Stand on   To hold one's course and speed.

Standing   Permanent.

Starboard   The right-hand side looking forward.

Starboard tack   Sailing with the wind blowing on the starboard side.

Start   To loosen.

Stave   To crush in.

Stays   Standing rigging of a mast in the fore-and-aft plane.

Steady   Order to a helmsman to stay on the course the vessel is on at the moment of the order being given.

Steer   To guide or direct.

Steerage way   To have enough movement through the water for the rudder to take effect.

Stem   The forward vertical timber or plate of a ship. Also to meet.

Step   The socket cut in the keelson to receive a mast heel or tongue. Smaller boats may have step on deck.

Stern   The after end of a vessel.

Sternboard   Lost ground when tacking up a narrow channel (see *make a sternboard*).

Sternpost   The aftermost vertical timber of a vessel.

Sternway   Movement through the water, stern first.

Stiff   Standing up well to the wind under canvas.

Stops   Pieces of rotten yarn used to secure a sail tightly about its own luff.

Storm   Force 10 to 11, Beaufort scale; wind of 48–65 nautical miles per hour.

Strand   A number of yarns twisted together in ropemaking.

Stream anchor   An anchor let go over the stern when mooring stem and stern in a tideway.

Stream, to   To cast overboard a log or an anchor buoy.

Strike   To lower down. Topmasts, upper spars, flags, etc. may be struck.

Strong wind   Force 6 and 7, Beaufort scale; wind of 22–33 nautical miles per hour.

Strop   A rope or metal band.

Strum box   A perforated drum or box placed at the bottom of the inlet pipe to the bilge pump to prevent paper, etc. clogging the pump.

Surge   To allow a rope to render round a revolving or stationary capstan, bollard, etc.

Swig   To take an extra pull on a halyard.

Swing ship   To turn a ship through all the points of the compass to ascertain the compass deviation.

Tabernacle   The housing in which the heel of a lowering mast rests.

Tabling   The double seam round the edges of a sail.

Tack   The foremost lower corner of a fore-and-aft sail. A board or leg (which see) when beating to windward—hence starboard tack, a board made with the wind on the starboard side of a vessel. The rope or purchase attached to the foremost lower corner of a sail.

Tack, to   To work a vessel to windward by sailing alternately closehauled with the wind on the starboard side and closehauled with the wind on the port side; to alter course through the wind when beating to windward; to change course from the port to the starboard tack, and vice versa.

Tackle   A combination of rope and chains; gear generally. A combination of pulley blocks forming a purchase.

Taffrail   The rail round the stern of the ship; the capping of the bulwarks on the stern.

Tail   A length of rope spliced on the blocks of a tackle.

Tail, to   To clap onto a rope; to attach another hawser to the end of one which is being paid out.

Take charge   To get out of control, especially sails or gear.

Take in   To furl and stow sails.

Take up   To shorten or tighten gear. Of gaping seams in planking, to close up tight when the boat is immersed in water and the wood has swelled.

Taking off   The steady decrease in the range and velocity of tides from springs to neaps.

Taut   Tight; stretched tightly under strain.

Tender   A small vessel, such as a yacht's dinghy, used to attend on her parent vessel.

Thimble   A grooved metal ring, circular or heart-shaped, used to line an eye in a rope.

Thole   Peg fitted in a rowing boat's gunwale to act as a fulcrum to the oar. Thole pin.

Thoroughfoot   To coil a rope down in figure-of-eight shaped flakes.

Throat   The end of a gaff or boom nearest to the mast; the upper inner corner of a gaffsail or spritsail.

Thumb cleat   A small projecting piece of wood secured to a spar to prevent a strop from slipping.

Thwarts   Rowers' seats running from side to side of an open boat.

Thwartships   see *athwart*.

Tidal streams   A periodic horizontal movement of the sea.

Tide The periodic vertical movement of the sea caused by solar and lunar attraction.

Tide rip or race Disturbed seas caused by tidal eddies or the passage of a tidal stream over an uneven or shallow bottom.

Tide-rode The situation of a ship anchored in a tideway when, the effect of the tide being greater than the effect of the wind, she lies head to tide.

Tiers, ties Short lengths of rope or canvas used to secure a furled sail to its spar.

Tight Free from leaks.

Tiller Wood or metal bar secured to the rudderhead by means of which a vessel is steered.

Timbers A collective name for the skeleton and unplanked frame of a yacht; the vertical frames or ribs of a yacht.

Tingle A patch piece of lead or copper put on the outside of a vessel over a hole or similar damage in the planking.

Toggle A small piece of wood used for securing a rope end to a small eye, for preventing a marlinespike hitch or a sheepshank from coming undone, etc.

Tonnage The measurement of a ship's internal capacity, calculated in various ways.

Top hamper Gear above decks.

Top To lift one end, e.g. of a boom; to fill up to the top.

Topping lift A rope which tops up one end of a spar and also takes the weight of the spar.

Topsail A sail set above the gaff sail on a fore-and-aft rigged vessel.

Tow To pull a vessel through the water.

Track To haul a vessel through the water using man-power or horse-power for the work.

Transom The stern planking of a square-sterned vessel.

Traveller A ring travelling along a spar and to which a sail is secured; by hauling this ring along the spar the sail is set close to the spar.

Trend Direction.

Trestletrees Pieces of timber at the hounds which support the crosstrees and topmast fid.

Triatic stay A stay connecting the foremast and the mainmast head in a schooner.

Trice To hoist up.

Tricing line A rope, one end of which is secured to the tack of the sail, rove through a block at the hounds or gaff jaws, used for tricing or trussing the tack of a loose-footed gaffsail (see *scandalize*).

Trim The horizontal equilibrium of a ship.

Trim, to To adjust sails by manipulating the sheets. To arrange cargo or ballast to affect trim.

Trimaran Three-hulled vessel.

Trip To catch a wave crest with the boom when running; to lift clear (e.g. to trip an anchor); to lift the topmast a little on its heel-rope to enable the fid to be withdrawn.

Tripping line An erroneous but frequently used name for an anchor buoy rope.

Truck Circular piece of wood at the masthead which contains sheaves for flag halyards.

Truss To brail up; to scandalize a gaff sail; to trice up.

Try To heave to.

Trysail A three-cornered sail usually part of a yacht's storm canvas and forming the after sail, spread when heaving to in heavy weather. Not set on a boom.

Turn To beat to windward; to tack.

Turn in To go below to sleep; to make an eye in the end of a rope round an object such as a deadeye.

Turn, to take a To pass a rope once or twice round anything; to secure round a cleat or bollard.

Ugly Threatening weather.

Unbend Undo; untie; cast off; remove sails from their yards, etc.

Unbitt To cast the upper securing turns of a cable off the bitts, leaving one riding turn on.

Under power The condition of a vessel when mechanical power is being used to propel her through the water.

Under-run To follow up the run of a rope with something underneath it; e.g. to under-run an anchor cable is to follow up the run of a cable by hauling it in over a small boat which moves out in the direction of the anchor; to separate or clear the legs or part of a purchase.

Under way Having no movement through the water but not anchored, aground or moored. Not to be confused with making way.

Unrig   To take the standing and running rigging and sails off a vessel; to dismantle something.

Unship   Remove; cast off.

Up helm   To put the tiller up to windward; an order resulting in the ship's head being turned away from the wind.

Vangs, vanes or whangs   Ropes controlling the lateral movement of the after end of a gaff or sprit.

Veer   A wind shift with the sun, clockwise in the N hemisphere. Of a ship's movement, to sheer away from. To pay out cable link by link, by reversing the drive of a capstan; to ease away slowly and steadily while retaining complete control.

Veer and haul   Literally to ease and then haul on a rope—generally used to express shifting opinions, fair-weather views, vacillation.

Wake   The disturbed water left behind in the path of a moving vessel.

Warp   A rope by which anything is hauled along; the rope cable of an anchor in small craft. Of sailcloth, the lengthwise measurement or threads.

Warp, to   To move a vessel forward by hauling on a hawser or warp attached to a mooring buoy or to posts on shore; of timber, to curl or lose shape.

Wash   The wave-form created by a boat moving through the water.

Watches   The division of a ship's company into suitable parts for general duty. See Appendix F.

Waterline (WL)   The horizontal plan of a ship on the level at which she floats. The length of a vessel between perpendiculars on the horizontal waterline plane. The ship's side at the level of the water.

Waterlogged   Full of water but still floating.

Way   Momentum, movement through the water. See *steerage way,* under way.

Wear   To go round stern to wind from the starboard tack to the port tack and vice versa, instead of through the wind (head to wind) as in tacking.

Weather   To windward, e.g. weather side, weather bow, weather roll, etc.

Weather helm   The necessity, in order to maintain a straight course, to keep the tiller a'weather because of the vessel's tendency to turn up into the wind. Such a craft is said to carry weather helm.

Weather bound   Unable to leave harbour, by reason of bad weather prevailing.

Weather eye open   To keep a good lookout to windward.

Weather shore   The land to windward of a vessel.

Weather tide, weather-going tide   A tidal stream setting to windward.

Weather, to   To pass safely to windward of something. To come safely through a gale.

Weeps   Red rust smears caused by the rusting of iron fastenings. Owner's euphemism for small leaks.

Weigh   To raise the anchor from the sea bottom.

Well   Cockpit, the sunk part of the deck in which the helmsman sits to steer; the lower part of the vessel's bilges.

Westering   Of the sun between noon and sunset.

Westing   Distance made good to the westward.

White horses   Breaking wave crests.

White squall   A sudden squall which whips the sea into a mass of foam.

Wholesome   Comfortable and seaworthy in a heavy way.

Wild   A vessel which steers badly.

Winch   A species of small windlass in which a drum is revolved by the action of a ratchet lever or bar.

Wind   Air in motion. Its force is measured in accordance with the Beaufort scale.

Wind-bound   Unable to proceed by reason of adverse winds.

Wind-rode   The position of a ship anchored in a tideway, when the strength of the wind being greater than that of the tide she lies head to wind.

Wind-sail   A canvas tube used to direct the wind into the body of the ship in hot weather.

Windlass   A machine of the wheel and axle order used for hauling in the chain cable, etc. It is operated by means of handspikes or, more usually, by a crank or bar.

Windward   On the side upon which the wind is blowing; the direction from which the wind is blowing.

With the sun   Clockwise in direction.

Withie   A willow; a stake or perch, sometimes used to beacon the navigable channel of a small river or creek.

Work a vessel   To handle or manoeuvre a vessel.

Work   To become slack or loose; of a ship's fabric, to strain open in a seaway. To sail, to keep moving, e.g. to work to windward.

Working gear   Gear or clothing in general use; the sails used by a ship when working to windward in ordinary weather.

Working staysail or foresail   One whose sheet travels across the deck on a horse.

Worm   To fill in the lay of a rope with small line in order to make a smoother, rounder surface forming and serving. Worming is done with the lay of a rope.

Wrack   Anything cast up on the shore and left behind by the receding tide.

Wreck   The destruction of a ship by the sea or by an accident, or what is left of a vessel after destruction has occurred.

Wring   To twist, to subject to twisting strain.

Yacht   A vessel used for pleasure only.

Yard   A spar suspended from a mast for the purpose of spreading the head of a sail.

Yardarm   The outer end of a yard, especially of a squaresail yard.

Yarn   A number of fibres of coir, sisal, hemp, cotton, etc. twisted together, usually right-handed.

Yaw   To swing or swerve from side to side of the course ordered, usually as a result of bad seamanship.

Yawl   A two-masted vessel, having a mainmast and a shorter mizzen mast, the latter stepped abaft the sternpost.

Yoke lines   Pieces of rope leading from each end of the rudder yoke for turning it and the rudder.

Young flood   The first movement of a flood tide.

Appendix B   Parts of a Yacht

The diagrams below show the parts of a yacht and the names by which they are called. It is important that these names should be learned as soon as possible as most are in constant use when sailing.

M

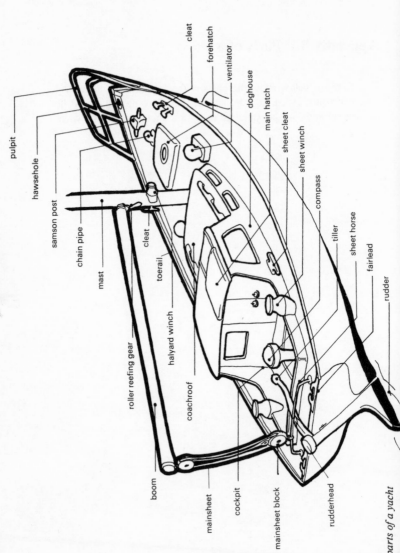

65 The parts of a yacht

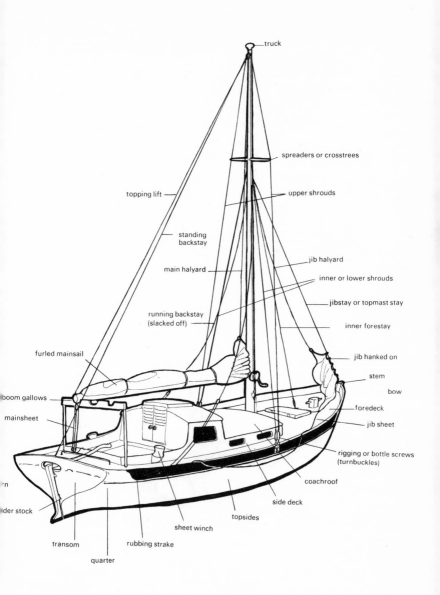

truck

spreaders or crosstrees

upper shrouds

topping lift

standing
backstay

jib halyard

main halyard

inner or lower shrouds

jibstay or topmast stay

running backstay
(slacked off)

inner forestay

furled mainsail

jib hanked on

stem

bow

boom gallows

foredeck

mainsheet

jib sheet

rigging or bottle screws
(turnbuckles)

coachroof

side deck

'n

ider stock

topsides

transom

sheet winch

rubbing strake

quarter

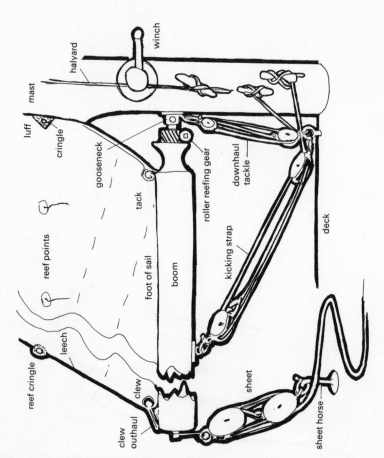

winch

halyard

mast

luff

cringle

gooseneck

tack

reef points

foot of sail

boom

roller reefing gear

downhaul

tackle

kicking strap

deck

reef cringle

leech

clew

clew
outhaul

sheet

sheet horse

66 Main boom

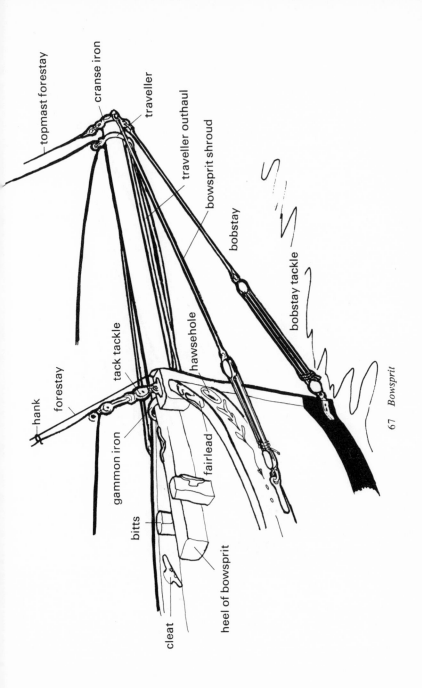

topmast forestay

cranse iron

traveller

traveller outhaul

bowsprit shroud

bobstay

bobstay tackle

hank

forestay

tack tackle

hawsehole

gammon iron

fairlead

bitts

cleat

heel of bowsprit

67   *Bowsprit*

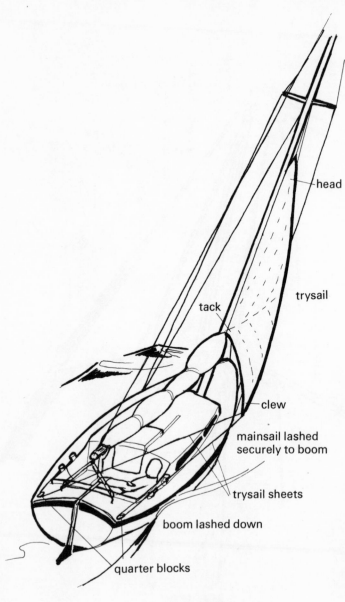

head

trysail

tack

clew

mainsail lashed
securely to boom

trysail sheets

boom lashed down

quarter blocks

68 *Trysail*

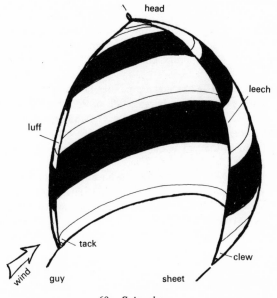

head

leech

luff

tack

clew

wind

guy

sheet

69 *Spinnaker*

Appendix C Knots

The number of possible knots and lashings are legion and several books have been devoted to the art. However, only a few knots are necessary for the novice, and an experienced crewman who can tie a dozen different knots is the exception. Some of the more useful knots are given below, and those which the novice must know are starred. All knots and splices to some extent lessen the strength of the rope.

Hitches A hitch is a knot used to secure a rope to another object such as a post or ring.

Half hitch A temporary knot which will hold if tension is kept on it.

Clove hitch* Used to make a painter fast to a post, to secure a burgee halyard to a burgee staff, or for tying ratlines. Can be made either over the top of a post or staff or tied around it.

Rolling hitch Used to tie a small line to a larger rope or spar (such as the gaff boom of a lugsail) where the pull is nearly parallel.

Fishermen's bend Not really a bend but a hitch. Used to tie a yacht's painter to a post or a warp to an anchor where a lot of jerking is expected. The end should be secured with a seizing in the case of an anchor.

Bends Bends are knots which are used to tie the ends of two free lines together.

Sheet bend To tie together two ends of ropes which are of different size and/or materials.

Double sheet bend A better bend to use when one rope is much larger than the other.

Reef knot* Not really a bend but a knot which is used to tie up a bundle. Should not be used to tie two ropes together which are subject to heavy strain as it can jam. A very useful knot for all lashing purposes. Tied the wrong way it becomes a granny knot, which may slip or jam. Used to tie reef points around the bundled sail.

Loops Loops are simply knots that can be used to make a loop at the end of a rope.

Bowline knot* A simple and efficient way to tie a fixed loop in the end of a rope so that it does not slip and is easy to undo. Used on bow and stern and other mooring lines, and can be used for many purposes. Note how similar it is to the sheet bend.

Stopper knots Stopper knots are made in the end of a rope to stop it running out through a hole or block.

Figure of eight knot* This is a simple knot used at the end of mainsail or headsail sheets so that they do not pull out through the sheet blocks.

Whippings Whippings are a tight binding of smaller lashing put round the end of a rope to prevent it unravelling.

Plain whipping A quick and simple whipping that can be put on without any tools. Will not take a lot of wear.

Sailmaker's whipping A much more effective whipping put on with a palm and needle.

Seizings Seizings are lashings on two ropes to hold them together.

Round seizing A simple method of lashing two ropes together, often used to make temporary eye in the end of a rope.

Racking seizing A more effective form of seizing where excessive tension is expected. Often used to make the eye in the middle of a pair of headsail sheets.

Splices Method of interweaving the strands of rope to join them or to make an eye, etc.

Short splice Used to join two ropes together. A strong method but results in the rope being thicker in way of the splice.

Eye splice The usual way to make a permanent eye in the end of a rope.

Ropes of man-made material Ropes made of plastics can be melted by heat and a match can be used to make the ends secure from unravelling. There are also plastic sheaths that can be melted over the ends to form whippings. Some of these ropes are specially woven so that other methods have to be used for splicing.

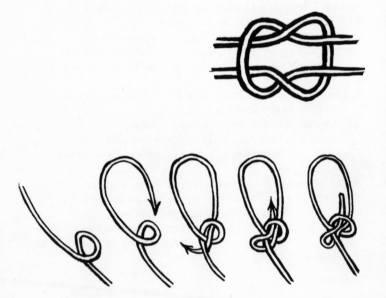

70 *Reef knot*
71 *Bowline*

72 *Figure of eight knot*
73 *To heave or cast the lead, secure yourself in the leeward shrouds. Tie the end of the lead line to some strong point nearby and coil the rest of the line into one hand ready to run. Hold the lead on a short scope (length) and swing it fore and aft, casting it into the sea ahead and to the side of the bow*

Appendix D   Further Reading

There are probably more books written about yachting than any other sport. The novice will find great difficulty in selecting suitable books for further study from the mass that are to be found in any good bookshop. Below are listed a limited number of books which are worth reading in order to broaden one's knowledge. This list is in no way complete nor is it exclusive, as there are many other books on these subjects which are as good and which some may consider better than those recommended.

Navigation
Coastwise Navigation, G C Watkins
Basic Coastal Navigation, Conrad Dixon
Little Ship Navigation, M J Rantzen

Seamanship
Cruising, J D Sleightholme
Cruising, P Heaton
At Home in Deep Water, Bruce Fraser
Heavy Weather Sailing, K Adlard Coles
The Sea Wife's Handbook, J Sleightholme

Knots
Knots and Splices, Cyrus Day
Your Book of Knots, P W Blandford
Brown's Knots and Splices, Capt. Jutsum

Meteorology
Instant Weather Forecasting, A Watts
Little Ship Meteorology, M J Rantzen

Cooking
Weekend Sailor's Cook Book, G Lewis
Gourmet in the Galley, F M Morrison
Cooking Afloat, Florence Hanbulot

General
ABC for Yachtsmen, J D Sleightholme
Flags and Signals, ed by R L Hewitt

Appendix E   Clothing and Personal Equipment

The problem of what clothing and equipment to take aboard is a very real one for a novice going on his first voyage and it is hoped that the lists given below will help him in selecting suitable things to take with him. It is difficult to make lists to suit every occasion, as personal taste, the length of the cruise, the time of year, the plans and standards of the skipper all affect the choice, to say nothing of the state of the crew's personal finances.

The lists below are for a period in excess of a week and are divided into *must, should* and *could have*. The novice would be ill-advised to go to sea without any of the *must* items and, always provided that there is adequate space aboard, those of the *should* category that he can obtain.

As previously stated oilskins are essential, but are expensive to buy. See if you can borrow from a friend, or perhaps the skipper may have a spare suit.

Remember that anything taken aboard may get salt water on it and may get bundled up and crushed in some locker, so do not take anything you value that could get permanently damaged. Stowage space is always limited and crews usually take more gear aboard than they really want or need.

A final reminder—do not pack gear into a suitcase but into a duffle bag, kit bag or grip that can be folded flat and stowed away.

Clothing, men

Foul weather	Must	Should	Could
1 suit of oilskins: high trousers and smock anorak	1		
1 so'wester, oilskin type			1
1 pair seaboots, short type with non-slip soles		1	
3 neck scarves, of terry towelling	2		1

Cold weather	Must	Should	Could
1 deck coat/duffle coat of wool		1	
1 pair strong gloves		1	
2 string vests or thick wool		2	+1
2 string pants or thick wool		2	+1
2 pairs seaboot stockings, oiled wool		1	+1
2 thick trousers, oiled wool	1	+1	
3 flannel shirts, thick as possible	1	+1	+1
3 thick sweaters, oiled wool	2	+1	
1 woolly cap		1	
1 track suit (in lieu of thick under-wear)	1		

Normal weather			
1 anorak/denim coat, spray-proofed		1	
3 denim trousers	1	+1	+1
1 deck shoes, non-slip canvas	1		
2 socks, medium weight	2		
2 shirts, medium weight	2		
2 sweaters, medium weight		1	+1
3 vests, normal weight	2	+1	
4 pants, normal weight	2	+2	

Fair weather			
2 shorts		1	+1
3 bathing shorts	1	+1	+1
3 thin shorts		2	+1
1 hat with brim		1	

Shore going			
1 reefer jacket, or suit in lieu		1	
2 white shirts		1	+1
2 pairs thin socks, black		2	
1 black or grey trousers		1	
1 pair shoes		1	
2 ties		1	+1
1 anorak or oilskin coat			1

176

Toilet articles   Must Should Could

shaving gear, toothbrush etc, washing
and hair gear

	Must	Should	Could
hand/face cream	1	+1	
sun oil	1	+1	
deodorant	1		

Miscellaneous

	Must	Should	Could
belts	1	+1	
hanks	6	+6	+6
Duffle or kit bag or grip	1		

Clothing, women

Foul weather

	Must	Should	Could
1 suit oilskins	1		
1 so'wester			1
1 pair sea boots, non-slip soles		1	
3 neck scarves, towelling	2	+1	

Cold weather

	Must	Should	Could
1 deck coat/duffle, wool		1	
1 pair gloves		1	
2 sets warm underwear, wool	2		+1
2 thick socks (men's seaboot type)	1		+1
3 thick trousers (one good for shore-going)	2	+1	
2 thick tights or long johns	1	+1	
3 thick sweaters (large to fit over others)	2	+1	
1 warm cap or scarf			1
1 track suit in lieu of 1 set warm underwear	1		

Normal weather

	Must	Should	Could
1 anorak, wind and showerproof		1	
2 trousers, demin or similar	2		
1 good shore wear trousers		1	
1 pair deck shoes, non-slip	1		

177

	Must	Should	Could
3 sweaters med. weight, 1 for shore wear	1	+2	
2 sets normal underwear	2		
2 head scarves, if worn			2
1 shoregoing dress or skirt (simple)		1	
1 shoregoing shoes (simple)		1	

Fair weather

	Must	Should	Could
2 bathing costumes or bikinis	1		+1
2 blouses (long shirt type best)		2	
1 towel for swimming		1	
1 swim hat, if worn			1

Personal gear

	Must	Should	Could
Washing things, usual toilet articles			
Towel	1	.	+1
Makeup but keep very simple			
1 large tin cold cream (seawater dries skin)		1	
1 hand cream		1	
1 shampoo (plastic pack best)			1

Miscellaneous

	Must	Should	Could
1 duffle or kitbag	1		
1 handbag (not too large and best soft, perhaps canvas)	1		
hanks or packet of tissues	6	+6	+6

Personal items and equipment

Men and Women

	Must	Should	Could
glasses (if normally used)	1		
dark glasses	1		
whistle	1		
clasp knife on lanyard	1		
hand torch	1		
wristwatch (waterproof)		1	spare
camera			1

178

	Must	Should	Could
transistor radio, tape recorder			1
(check with skipper)			
passport	1		
travellers' cheques		1	
chequebook		1	
foreign money		1	
bankers' card		1	
stationery, etc			

Appendix F   Watch Systems

On any voyage that lasts more than half a day it is normal and wise to set watches and to see that those off watch are resting. The programme for these watches will be organised by the skipper allowing for the following factors:

Total number of crew available to stand a watch bearing in mind that it may be advisable in certain circumstances to exclude the skipper and sometimes the navigator and/or cook.
The knowledge, skill, and strength of individual crew members.
The expected duration of the voyage allowing for possible delays.
The weather expected to be encountered.
The minimum number of crew necessary on watch which will enable the yacht to be kept sailing safely.

Watches can be organised in a number of different ways and sometimes one arrangement is used during daylight and another at night.

Traditional or naval watches

This system is still used on naval and merchant service vessels and is bound up with the traditional method of indicating the time by strokes on a bell every half hour. It is often used on larger yachts where there are enough crew available to form three separate watches. In this case a crewman is on deck for four hours and off watch for eight hours. Note that the two dog (dodge) watches of two hours each ensure that each crew has a different period to stand watch each day.

Bells are rung in pairs for the hours, with a single stroke after the half hour; the maximum number is eight bells which occurs every four hours.

12 noon to 4 p.m.		
8 bells to 8 bells	Afternoon watch	4 hours
4 p.m. to 6 p.m.		
8 bells to 4 bells	First dog watch	2 hours

6 p.m. to 8 p.m.		
4 bells to 8 bells	Second dog watch	2 hours
8 p.m. to 12 midnight		
8 bells to 8 bells	First night watch	4 hours
12 midnight to 4 a.m.		
8 bells to 8 bells	Mid-watch	4 hours
4 a.m. to 8 a.m.		
8 bells to 8 bells	Morning watch	4 hours
8 a.m. to 12 noon		
8 bells to 8 bells	Forenoon watch	4 hours

Three hour watch system

In the three hour watch system the day is divided into seven 3-hour periods and two of $1\frac{1}{2}$ hours to ensure daily rotation of duties. Alternatively it can be divided into six 3-hour and one 6-hour period. This is a good system when only one crew is on deck as three hours on the wheel is about all the normal person can do efficiently. With enough crew to divide into three watches it will give three hours' duty followed by six hours' rest.

Two hour watch system

With small crews and bad weather it may sometimes be necessary to use this system giving two hours on duty and four hours' rest, as steering in heavy weather is very tiring.

Scandinavian or six and four hour watch system

In this system there is a watch from 6 a.m. to noon and another from noon to 6 p.m. both six hours in duration, the night being divided into three watches of four hours each. This is a popular system where more than one person is in a watch so that they can relieve each other at the wheel. It is self rotating daily with either two or three watches.

There are a number of variations based on the above systems, sometimes incorporating one system for daylight and another for night-time use.

181

Appendix G   Sounding with Lead and Line

Most yachts are now equipped with electronic echo sounders which will give a constant reading of the amount of water under a yacht as it sails along. These instruments are invaluable but, as with any electronic equipment on a yacht, they can go wrong, usually at some crucial moment when the skipper wants to know the depth of water badly. It is then that knowledge of and skill with a lead and line is vital. In addition soundings taken with an armed lead (the bottom of the lead filled with tallow) will bring up a sample of the bottom which on occasions can be invaluable in identifying where the yacht is.

Casting or heaving the lead

Stand between the leeward shrouds, and secure yourself with a line so that your hands are free. Tie the end of the lead line to a strong point and coil the rest in the hand so that it will run out easily over the fingertips. Hold this coil in the forward hand, which should be ahead of the forward shroud so that the shoulder rests against the shroud to give stability. With the other hand hold the lead on the end of about three feet of line and swing it in a fore-and-aft direction taking care not to damage the hull. When sufficient amplitude has been obtained let it go forward to fall into the sea some yards ahead and to one side of the yacht's course, while allowing the line to run out freely.

Sounding

As the yacht approaches the place where the lead hit the bottom take in the slack and at the exact moment when you are level with the place and the line is vertical lift the lead a few inches and lower again, keeping the line taut, and as it touches the bottom read the measurement. Call out the reading so that the skipper can hear. Now recoil the line ready for another cast. Sounding with a lead and line can be a wet and exhausting process if kept up for any length of time and reliefs should accordingly be arranged. It is almost impossible to use a lead and line without getting wet so oilskins should be worn if more than one cast is necessary.

Marks and deeps

A lead line is marked as shown below at certain places. These are called marks and indicate by the type and colour of the mark how many fathoms they are from the lead. As these marks do not appear at every fathom there are unmarked places, the deeps.

Fathoms	Mark/Deep	Type of marking
0	Bottom of lead	
1	Deep 1	
2	Mark 2	Two leather strips
3	Mark 3	Three leather strips
4	Deep 4	
5	Mark 5	White cotton rag
6	Deep 6	
7	Mark 7	Red wool bunting or rag
8	Deep 8	
9	Deep 9	
10	Mark 10	Leather with hole in it
11	Deep 11	
12	Deep 12	
13	Mark 13	Blue serge or three leather strips (same as 3 fathoms)
14	Deep 14	
15	Mark 15	White cotton rag (same as 5 fathoms)
17	Mark 17	Red wool bunting
20	Mark 20	Cord with two knots

Note that the marks are designed so that they can be distinguished by feel at night. If it is very dark it may be necessary to measure from the rail and adjust afterwards by subtracting the height of the rail above water. Make sure the skipper knows in advance which figure you are reporting.

Reporting

The leadsman should report as follows:

When the depth corresponds to a mark, 'By the mark five', or which mark it is.

When the depth corresponds to a deep, 'By the deep six', or which deep it is.

When the depth falls between fathom marks or deeps, 'And a half seven' or 'Half less eight'. Both are the same.

Note that the actual or nearest depth in fathoms is always the last word. It would be advisable to check with your skipper first before using these reports to see if he knows about marks and deeps, etc. Most skippers will be a little hazy due to lack of practice.

Appendix H   The Rules of the Road at Sea

All members of a yacht's crew should have a basic knowledge of the International Regulations for Preventing Collisions at Sea. It is not necessary to know all the rules, nor is it necessary to know the rules in detail, as many are framed for the use of large merchant vessels or for very rare occasions which are not likely to be encountered by a yacht.

The most important rules are listed below in a simplified form. Those which are starred *must* be known and understood by the good crewman. The rule numbers in the right-hand column are from the complete version so that if any further information is required it will be a simple matter to look it up.

Notes

An electric torch and an oil hand lantern are considered to be interchangable, but their use is not advised as they tend to produce ambiguous lights. This is due to the difficulty in keeping the coloured sectors correctly oriented to the fore-and-aft line of the boat showing the light.

Port and starboard side lights can be combined in one lamp or torch, or two separate lamps. These are located normally on the sides of a vessel but in some yachts can be placed on the bow. In all cases they show from dead ahead over an arc of $112\frac{1}{2}°$ to either side, red to port (the left side facing forward) and green to starboard.

The stern light or torch shows white over an arc of 135° astern, which completes the 360° so that one light is visible from any direction. When passing a vessel, as one light vanishes the neighbouring one will become visible. There is a small overlap due to the width of the beam. For instance, when red and green lights are seen at the same time the vessel is pointing straight towards you.

A sailing vessel under power counts as a power vessel with regard to lights, signals and rights of way.

185

Lights and Shapes

Type	Day	Night	Rule
Small boat under oars	—	White torch	7(f)
Sailing boat less than 40ft under way	—	Red and green torch and white torch astern *or* Red and green side lights and white stern light	7(d) 10(b) 2(a) (iv, v) 10(a)
Power boat less than 40ft under way	—	Red and green torch and white torch *or* Red and green side lights and white steaming light on the mast and white stern light	7(c) 10(b) 2(a) (iv) & (v) 2(a) (i) 10(a)
*Sailing vessel over 40ft under way	—	Red and white side lights and white stern light *plus* Red over green lights on mast, both visible 360° (not compulsory)	5(a), 2(a) 10(a) 5(b)
*Power vessels over 65ft	—	Red and white side lights white steaming light on mast white stern light *plus* White steaming light on an aftermast (not compulsory)	2(a) (iv, v) 2(a) (i) 10(a) 2(a) (ii)
*Power vessels over 150ft	—	Red and white side lights two white steaming lights stern light	2(a) (iv, v) 2(a) (i, ii) 10(a)
Power vessels towing	Black diamond	All normal lights plus two white lights vertically on the mast	3(c)
	vessel towed, black diamond	A third white light if tow over 600ft	3(a), 5(d)

Type	Day	Night	Rule
*Vessel not under command (broken down or no-one on watch)	Two black shapes vertically	Two red lights vertically	4(a)
Vessel engaged in underwater work	Two red balls with black diamond between, vertically	One red light above and one below, white light on mast	4(c)
Power pilot vessel on station	(Identifiable by white over red pilot's flag)	Red light below white light on mast All normal lights	8(a) (i)
*Vessels trawling	Black shape or two cones point to point	Green light above white light on mast All normal lights if moving	9(c) (i, h) 9(e)
*Vessels fishing	Black shape or two cones point to point Cone point up in direction of gear if over 500ft away	Red light above white light on mast If gear over 500ft away white light in direction of gear All normal lights if moving	9(d, h) 9(f) 9(h)
*Vessel at anchor	Black ball	White light in bows Over 150ft long another in the stern but lower	11(a, c) 11(b)
Vessel aground	Three black balls vertically	Anchor lights and not under command lights	11(e)
*Sailing vessel also being propelled by power	Black cone point down	All normal lights plus a steaming light on the mast	14

Sound Signals

In conditions of bad visibility

Type	Signal	Rule
*Vessel under 40ft Rowing boat	Some efficient sound every minute	15(c) (ix)
*Power vessel over 40ft making way (moving through water)	Long blast on whistle every two minutes (—)	15(c) (i)
Power vessel over 40ft under way (but not moving through the water)	Two long blasts on whistle every two minutes (— —)	15(c) (ii)
*Sailing vessel on starboard tack on port tack running	One short blast on foghorn every minute (·) Two short blasts on foghorn every minute (· ·) Three short blasts on foghorn every minute (· · ·)	15(c) (iii)
*Vessel at anchor	Ring bell for 5 seconds every minute	15(c) (iv)
Vessel over 350ft at anchor	Ring bell for 5 seconds every minute on foredeck and gong for 5 seconds aft	15(c) (iv)
Vessel at anchor and in danger of being run down	One short, one long, on short blast on whistle or foghorn (· — ·) (Morse R)	15(c) (iv)
Vessel not under command or engaged in underwater work	One long blast followed by two short blasts every minute (— · ·)	15(c) (v)
Vessel towing and vessel towed	One long blast followed by three short blasts every minute (— · · ·)	15(c) (vi)
Vessel aground	At anchor signal preceded and followed by three strokes	15(c) (vii)

Type	Signal	Rule
Fishing vessel	Vessel not under command signal (— · ·)	15(c) (viii)
Pilot vessel	Normal signal plus four short blasts (· · · ·)	15(c) (x)

Note—A short blast is about one second long and a long blast is six seconds.

Sound Signals for Power Vessels

Manoeuvring Action

Action	Signal	Rule
*I am altering course to starboard	One short blast on whistle (·)	28(a)
*I am altering course to port	Two short blasts on whistle (· ·)	28(a)
*My engines are going astern	Three short blasts on whistle (· · ·)	28(a)
*Are you taking enough action to avoid me?	Five short blasts on whistle (· · · · ·)	28(b)
I am approaching an obscured bend in a narrow channel	One long blast on whistle (—)	25(b)

Rights of way

Situation	Action	Rule
*Two sailing vessels approaching each other on opposite tacks	Vessel on port tack gives way	17(a) (i)

189

Situation	Action	Rule
*Two sailing vessels approaching each other on the same tack	Vessel to windward gives way	17(a) (ii)
Two power vessels approaching each other end on (bow to bow). *Note:* this does not apply to vessels which if they hold their course will pass clear of each other on either side	Both alter to starboard and pass port to port (*viz.* driving on the Continent)	18(a)
Two power vessels crossing on collision course	Vessel which has the other on her starboard side gives way	19
*Sailing and power vessel on collision course (except in confined waters or when overtaking)	Power vessel gives way	20(a)
*Sailing and power vessel in confined waters (narrow channel)	Sailing vessel gives way	20(b)
Vessel that has the right of way	Stands on at a steady course and speed, only altering at last moment to avoid collision	21
Vessel that has to take avoiding action	Takes positive action, if necessary slows up or goes astern in good time, and if possible avoids crossing ahead	22
Vessel overtaking another	Overtaking vessel keeps clear	24(a)
Power vessel in narrow channel	Keeps to starboard side (*viz.* driving on the right)	25(a)
*Power vessel under 65ft in a narrow channel	Gives way to larger vessels	25(c)
*Power and sailing vessels approaching a vessel fishing	All vessels keep clear of fishing vessels	26

Note—A sailing vessel under power counts as a power vessel.

190

Mnemonics

The following mnemonics may help you to remember some of the rules.

Port and starboard Channel marks	There is some *red port left* in the bottle. Left home, Cones left. Home for the night, Cones on the right. There's port left, sir, But only in cans.
Sailing ships on opposite tacks	The ship that has the wind to *port* *Must keep well clear is what we're taught.* *If the wind's on the right* we're all right (jack).
Power vessels approach- ing bow to bow	When you see both lights ahead Starboard wheel, and show your *red*. (for wheel steering) Port your helm and show your *red*. (for tiller steering)
Power vessels passing	Green to green, or red to red Perfect safety, go ahead.
Power vessels crossing	If to your starboard *red* appear 'Tis your duty to keep clear, To act as judgment says is proper, To port or starboard, back or stop her! But when on your port is seen A steamer's starboard light or *green* There's not so much for you to do, For *green* to port keeps clear of you.
Good lookout	Both in safety and in doubt Always keep a good lookout. In danger, with no room to turn, Ease her! Stop her! Go astern!